The International

ADJUSTMENT
MECHANISM

Proceedings of a

CONFERENCE

Held at

MELVIN VILLAGE, NEW HAMPSHIRE

OCTOBER 8 – 10, 1969

Sponsored by

THE FEDERAL RESERVE BANK OF BOSTON

THE FEDERAL RESERVE BANK OF BOSTON
CONFERENCE SERIES

FOREWORD

The papers included in this volume were presented at a conference sponsored by the Federal Reserve Bank of Boston in October 1969.

This conference was the second of a planned series covering a wide range of financial and monetary problems. The proceedings of the first of the series, *Controlling Monetary Aggregates,* is also available. A third conference, focusing on problems of state and local government finance, will be held in June 1970, and, like the first two sessions, will bring together a distinguished group of academicians and financial practitioners.

The past year has been one of lively debate and important decisions concerning the international adjustment mechanism. It is hoped the publication of these proceedings will make a useful contribution to the continuing discussion and the related policy decisions in this area.

Frank E. Morris
President

Boston, Massachusetts

March, 1970

Second Printing, 7-70-10M
Third Printing, 11-71-5M
Fourth Printing, 5-73-5M

CONTENTS

The International
ADJUSTMENT
MECHANISM

PANEL

The International Adjustment Mechanism

RICHARD E. CAVES

In facing the topic assigned to me for this opening session, I was puzzled about how to strike out in the vast territory laid open for invasion, if not for conquest. On the one hand, I could take the utopian stance of announcing what would, in uncompromising terms, be a good, true, and proper international monetary mechanism. I have never been a very good utopian. I would be a better bank clerk. Furthermore, in noting the list of distinguished gentlemen who will be following me, I felt that sufficient utopian proposals might be forthcoming therefrom, and that I should perhaps take a somewhat more grey, gradualistic approach to the subject. So I shall devote my time to some remarks on the international adjustment mechanism, treating it as a question of whether or not a market mechanism of adjustment exists under fixed exchange rates, and raise a few issues about sources and sizes of disturbance to the system. We are all familiar with the underlying theoretical models. My concern is with the factual evidence which they designate as necessary to a choice among the major alternative ways of managing our international monetary affairs. The distinguished papers prepared for this conference will review the major proposals — float, crawl, band and the like. What do we know about the mechanism of adjustment that bears on the choice among these proposals?

Forces of Adjustment under a Fixed Exchange Rate

As a useful starting point, consider the forces adjusting an industrial country's balance under a fixed exchange rate. The textbooks describe two of them to us. In a strict Keynesian model of income-flow adjustments, a decline in exports ultimately causes a fall in imports although in all probability not enough to eliminate the disequilibrium. This familiar mechanism of adjustment ought to work in the right direction, but not by exactly the right amount.

Mr. Caves is Professor of Economics, Harvard University, Cambridge, Massachusetts.

Much interest in recent years has focused upon a more strictly monetary mechanism of adjustment. When a country has a balance of payments deficit, it will by definition be reducing its total privately-held asset stock, in the process of paying for the excess of purchases over sales. Its asset stock falls, its total financial assets relative to its level of current expenditure fall, and we may expect the level of expenditures to be reduced and the balance of payments pressed back toward equilibrium. The reduction in the stock of assets relative to the level of expenditure, and the fall in the price of internationally immobile relative to internationally mobile assets — as Professor Scitovsky has recently reminded us — ought to eliminate balance-of-payments disequilibria under fixed exchange rates, and without corrective government action.

The broad impression that one gets from discussions of these mechanisms of income and asset adjustment is that they are either weak or get short-circuited by government action. I would like to make some suggestions about the empirical status of these mechanisms of adjustment, on the view that their weaknesses in operation may tell us a lot about the case for reforming the system to give more play to the price mechanism of adjustment than does the Bretton Woods regime of the adjustable peg. Although my major argument will be that rapid growth in the sources and sizes of disturbances has been the principal enemy of these adjustment mechanisms, something should be said first about the role of government interferences to jam their operation. The role of government full-employment policy in short-circuiting the operation of these mechanisms is now commonplace knowledge. I am impressed, though, about the importance to one's preferences about the international monetary system of the answer to the following question: Do you or do you not believe in a relation of the Phillips Curve-type as dominating economic policy in the short run? If you feel that the rate of inflation and the level of employment cannot be disconnected from one another, then with a fixed exchange rate the number of policy instruments is inadequate to attain our objectives concerning employment, the price level, and the balance of payments. If you feel, however, that there is not a locked-in Phillips Curve relation and that the level of unemployment and the rate of increase of domestic prices can be separated with the armament of policy instruments now available, then the argument for flexible exchange rates to overcome a shortage of policy instruments is no longer necessarily compelling. Thus one's views on the need for greater exchange-rate flexibility tend to depend heavily on its necessity as a means of securing an adequate number of policy instruments.

Changing Patterns of International Transactions

Be that as it may, I would now urge that the changing patterns of international transactions on current and capital accounts reveal a great increase in the size and the sources of disturbance that may impinge on an industrial country's *ex ante* balance-of-payments position. Let me remind you of just a few of them. On the current account side, over the last decade we have observed a great increase in trade among the industrial countries, involving an increasingly fine differentiation of the industrial goods that they trade with one another. This has inevitably increased the price elasticities governing the current account. The result, of course, is that a given change in a country's price level then causes a much larger disequilibrium in its current account than if this development had not occurred.

The international corporation has made the location of production increasingly sensitive to the level of factor cost at the going exchange rate, and this also tends to increase the elasticities and thus the size of disturbance to the foreign balance that can follow a disturbance to the domestic price level. I have been impressed by Richard Cooper's argument that the transformation possibilities of individual industrial countries are becoming increasingly similar to one another, and that capital tends to flatten out natural advantages based on labor or land, making countries more closely competitive with one another. This also portends larger disturbances to the current-account balance as a result of any given domestic development.

This is all *a priori* reasoning about price elasticities; what about the statistical evidence? What are the econometricians saying these days? My allotted time does not allow a comprehensive survey of this field, but my reading supports an increasing conviction that the elasticities are high, and that despite some lags they do come through in a reasonable period of time. The econometricians are, of course, better at thinking up reasons about why their estimates are biased downward than they are at producing unbiased estimates. But putting together these two sources of econometric evidence — the actual and *a prioristic* — I think that is where one comes out.

On the current-account side I suggested that sources of increased disturbance overwhelm the capacity of income or monetary mechanisms to adjust to them without exchange-rate changes. What about the capital account? The same story can be told there. In the last 10 years it has seemed that every year — every month perhaps — some new category of international financial transactions has been devised or developed. Repeatedly the consciousness of the profitability of some international capital transaction has impinged on a new class of American or European lenders or borrowers. These innovations and discoveries are written in recent financial history — U.S. direct investment, the Euro-dollar market, long-term U.S. commercial bank loans, Euro-bonds, the discovery of the U.S. stock market by Europeans — one development after another that might be described as some set of asset holders recognizing a new possibility for profitable diversification of their portfolios. Where is this to end? How many more new forms can be invented?

Forecasting Innovation

The forecasting of innovation is always a difficult matter, but the point is that these possibilities of increasing interpenetration in financial markets mean much higher elasticities of flows of capital in response to differentials among countries in yields on assets. Of course, it is not just a matter of increasing sensitivity of capital flows to what you might call ordinary commercial-yield considerations. It is also a question of the sensitivity of capital flows to exchange-rate expectations, a constant worry under the adjustable peg.

Here again, I think, a learning process can be clearly detected. Many of my British friends have said that the British man in the street has, as a result of recurrent sterling crises, become conscious of the possible profitability of converting his liquid assets into something that is not sterling. When the whole domestic money supply is ready to take flight at the thought of a devaluation, then one has, I think, an impressive potential for disturbances in the system.

What about the hard quantitative evidence on the capital accounts, comparable to the elasticity evidence about trade flows? What is available is very persuasive. My own research on Canada in the last few years has suggested that, during the period of the flexible exchange rate, both short- and long-term portfolio capital flows to Canada were extremely sensitive to yield differentials, and that this sensitivity increased substantially over the 1950's and early 1960's. They were, I might mention, also highly sensitive in a stabilizing way to movements of the Canadian exchange rate; that is, the tendency of private capital flows to stabilize the fluctuating Canadian dollar was very strong.

My remarks have been aimed toward suggesting that, perhaps, the apparent inadequacies of income and monetary mechanisms of adjustment under fixed exchange rates may be traced to government policy decisions and to the constraints of domestic policy. There is a crucial question of whether we really are short of policy instruments. Secondly, the development of international transactions among the industrial nations has proceeded in a way that tends to enlarge disturbances to the balance of payments, and make them much more difficult to cope with under a fixed exchange rate.

PANEL

MILTON FRIEDMAN

The title of this session on the international adjustment mechanism is a sign, in my opinion, of enormous progress in the discussion
of problems of international monetary arrangements. The great
defect in most of the discussions, over most of the nearly two
decades that I have now followed them, is concentration on what are
really peripheral issues of liquidity and confidence, rather than on
the fundamental issue of what is the adjustment mechanism. So I
want to congratulate the Federal Reserve Bank of Boston for starting
our session with a discussion of the international adjustment mechanism.

Having gotten to that central problem, the next stage is to
complicate it a little by being a little more sophisticated about it.
Adjustment to what? Broadly speaking — and this is obviously an
oversimplification as any such statements must be — there are two
classes of things to which adjustment is required. There are adjustments to monetary disturbances and there are adjustments to real
disturbances, and they raise rather different problems. For example,
Dick Caves, in his discussion, spoke about sources of disturbances.
He spoke about what he regarded as increasing elasticities in trade
movements and in capital movements as meaning that the system was
subject to greater sources of disturbances. One could take exactly the
same evidence as meaning that the system has a more sensitive and an
improved adjustment mechanism. Which it is depends on what kind
of a disturbance you are thinking of. From the point of view of a
government that would like to inflate or deflate, the greater sensitivity of flows of trade and of capital is a source of disturbance. But
from the point of view of how the world monetary and economic
systems can adapt to changes in real conditions — the changes in the
comparative advantage of one place over another, or other similar
real conditions — the factors that Caves cites represent an improved
capacity to smooth the adjustment process. What I would like to do
in my few minutes here is to discuss what the adjustment mechanism

Mr. Friedman is Paul Snowden Russell Distinguished Service Professor of Economics,
University of Chicago, Chicago, Illinois.

has in fact been up to date, and then make a few comments about where it is going, leaving almost entirely unsaid where it ought to go.

Disturbances from Differential Degrees of Inflation

What has the adjustment mechanism been? It is common to emphasize, as Dick Caves did, differential degrees of inflation; to say that, under a system of fixed exchange rates, the adjustment mechanism involves pressure on countries in surplus to inflate more than countries showing a deficit. That is true; that has been a part of the adjustment mechanism. But, it's worth emphasizing, that differential inflation has also been a major source of the need for an adjustment mechanism. We have to distinguish between differential inflation that has been a response to balance-of-payments problems, and that has been a source of balance-of-payments problems. Milton Gilbert distinguished between two categories of countries; he distinguished between those countries that did and those that did not have a capacity for monetary discipline. The Bretton Woods distinction was very different. It was between those countries that had a reasonable capacity for monetary discipline and those countries that had an unreasonable capacity for monetary discipline. Many of the problems of this era have been produced not by the lack of effectiveness of differential degrees of inflation as an adjustment mechanism, but by the disturbances arising out of differential degrees of inflation. So differential degrees of inflation have been both adjustment mechanism and also a major source of disturbance.

Variations in Direct Controls over Trade and Payments

A second adjustment mechanism has been variations in direct controls over trade and payments. I think it is easy to underestimate how important a role changes in the degree of control over trade and payments have played in the adjustment process. As we all know, we came out of the post-war period with a "dollar shortage" that it was said was going to last indefinitely. At that time countries other than the United States had extensive trade controls and payments restrictions. The United States was easing up sharply on its restrictions. In the course of the swing from the dollar shortage to the dollar surplus, you had a major swing in the character and location of restrictions on trade and payments. The United States moved toward greater restrictions on trade and payments; most of the rest of the world moved toward lesser restrictions on trade and payments. So that over this period of 20 or 30 years a great role was played in the adjustment process by variations in trade controls.

Exchange Rate Changes

Thirdly, and this is the point that I want to emphasize most, in my opinion the major adjustment mechanism in the post-war period has been exchange rate changes. Dick Caves talks about the adjustments with exchange rates fixed. But the fact of the matter is that exchange rates have *not* been fixed. In an article written by Margaret DeVries and published in the *IMF Staff Papers* in November 1968, she examines what has happened to exchange rates in developing countries, distinguishing between their experience and the experience of what she calls "the more developed" countries. If I take only her 21 more-developed countries, so that I leave out most of those countries Milton Gilbert was referring to as having no capacity for monetary discipline, only three of them had either no change or an appreciation in the par value. Only the United States and Japan had no change. Germany had an appreciation. Eighteen of the 21 countries had a depreciation in their exchange rates vis-à-vis the dollar. Of those 18, 6 had a depreciation of less than 30 percent, and 12 out of the 21 — or more than half — had a depreciation of more than 30 percent. Much of the discussion about the process of adjustment in the post-war period reminds me of the man who discovered at the age of 70 that he had been speaking prose all of his life. We keep on talking about what are the adjustment mechanisms with exchange rates fixed, when the basic fact of the matter is that exchange rates have not been fixed, that exchange rates varied a great deal, and that they probably have played the major role in the adjustment mechanism in the post-war period. If you consider these depreciations of 30 or more percent, I wonder if you can find any cases at all of differential degrees of inflation that have been part of an adjustment process and that have been of anything like that magnitude. The large differential degrees of inflation have been sources of disturbance, not adjustment. Those differential degrees of inflation that have contributed to adjustments have been at the most of the order of 3, 4 or 5 percent differential. There is the Japanese case. From time to time, Japan has unquestionably used differential degrees of inflation as an adjustment mechanism. But the differential is of far smaller magnitude than the kind of exchange rate changes that have occurred.

The key basic fact that I think ought to be in the forefront of every such discussion as this one is that there is in fact only one effective adjustment mechanism to disturbances of the kind that have been experienced — namely, to disturbances arising primarily out of differential monetary behavior. That adjustment mechanism, the one we have been using, and the one we are going to keep on using, is exchange rate changes. There isn't anything else. The real question of policy is not, "Should exchange rate changes be used as an adjustment mechanism?" The real question of policy is, "How do you use exchange rate changes?" Do you use them as we have been doing by permitting difficulties to accumulate until they are major and then have a big change so that there is a crisis every time there's a change involving a major country? Or do we try to adapt our protestations and our professions to what really is going on and have a mechanism of changing exchange rates which is smoother, more gradual, which will occur more nearly automatically, and will involve fewer crises?

Need for Smoother Adjustments

That is the real issue and it seems to me that any discussion of whether you ought to have a world with a single money, or a single set of rates of exchange, is, in Dick Caves' terms, "utopian." I am utopian. I would like to see a world with a single money. Unlike Mr. Kindleberger, I would like to see it *without* a central monetary authority. But if we are going to talk about what are the realistic and the important alternatives facing the world today, there is no possibility, as I see it, of an adjustment mechanism in the near future that does not involve exchange rate changes — just as any proper description of the past 20 years must assign to exchange rate changes a major role in the adjustment mechanism.

Having said this, we can go on and ask the question: Given that major reliance on discontinuous, occasionally large changes in exchange rates has been the adjustment mechanism, what is happening now? Let me put one thing aside — the creation of SDR's. In my opinion, that is not going to alter the adjustment mechanism in any important way. It is going to have negligible effects on the character of the adjustment process. Its major effect will be to make the world price level somewhat higher than it otherwise would be. The SDR's are a subject for another discussion, and I don't mean to digress by going to them. I only want to express, and you'll pardon me if limitations of time make me do it very dogmatically, my own personal opinion that, whatever their merits may be for other purposes, they have little relation to an improved adjustment mechanism, because the problem of an adjustment mechanism is not a problem of reserves. It's a problem of adapting prices, exchange rates, real flows, and so on to shifts in other countries' monetary policies and to shifts in real circumstances underlying international trade.

A more important change currently taking place is a wider recognition of the point I have been stressing — that exchange rates are in fact the only available major mechanism at the moment to counteract monetary sources of disturbances. This is taking the form of a much greater interest by a wide range of people — both official and unofficial — in mechanisms for smoother flexibility. I think the experience of the German mark in the past few weeks is a fascinating episode and an important episode. In the climate of opinion among governmental officials of 10 years ago, that kind of a development would not have occurred. Germany would not have floated the mark. From my jaundiced point of view, the best thing would be if the Germans, seeing how well the floating rate works for three weeks, decided that it might not be bad for another three weeks, another three weeks, and another three weeks. We might in that way slip into a Canadian flexible exchange rate. But I am not very optimistic that that will happen. The desire on the part of central banks to play an important part in the international monetary mechanism is too strong, I believe, to be frustrated by the mere fact that a floating rate works very well. And, consequently, I feel very confident in the prediction that Germany will establish a new par in the not too distant future. But I think the experience that Germany has had may set an example and may encourage a wider range of countries — hopefully not only countries whose rates will float up — to experiment with the possibility of using gradual changes in exchange rates instead of abrupt ones.

Personally, as a matter of prediction, I find it hard to believe that there will be any international agreement on a gliding parity or any other automatic mechanism. I see as more likely a gradual introduction by individual countries, on their own say-so, of devices such as the one the Germans have just adopted. I had rather supposed that Germany, for example, instead of doing what she just did — which I think is splendid — might experiment with the gliding parity by appreciating the German mark on an announced basis of 1 percent a month for 10 months, or something like that. I think gliding parities of that kind will be experimented with by individual countries because they offer to monetary authorities a kind of half-way house between the complete flexibility of a free market on the one hand — desirable as that might be from my point of view, it is not from theirs — and on the other this awful business of holding and holding and holding to the last gasp and then having to make a big change.

PANEL

MILTON GILBERT

Instead of discussing the international adjustment mechanism in general terms, I would like to summarize how it has seemed to me to have operated in practice over the two decades that I have been concerned with it.

I may preface my remarks with two general points. Firstly, automatic adjustment has not been the major factor in securing reasonable external balance; deliberate policy actions to manage both the domestic economic situation and the balance of payments itself have been constantly required to make the adjustment mechanism work over a sufficient range. Secondly, to opt rigidly for either flexible rates or fixed rates has seemed to me to overgeneralize. As any theoretical model must be a simplification of reality, it is easy to construct a variety of plausible models. The real problem in dealing with practical cases of imbalance is to decide upon what model and what policy instruments are appropriate to the case at hand.

One can divide the countries of the world roughly into two groups: countries that have a reasonable capacity for monetary discipline and those that seem to have limited capacity for it. I will concentrate on the first group, because I do not know what to do about the second. Their real failure is in the exercise of political authority, and until that is corrected most of them would probably be better off not pegging the rate of exchange.

Adjustment Process in France, Germany, and Spain

Among the countries of the first group a disequilibrium in the balance of payments has arisen rather frequently over the years. Once the realignment of currencies in 1949 was out of the way, however, most of the imbalances that arose were of the sort that could be corrected by appropriate monetary and fiscal policy, with maybe a few extra gadgets — like managing the rate of borrowing or lending abroad, or temporary use of direct controls. The adjustment

Mr. Gilbert is Economic Adviser, Bank for International Settlements, Basle, Switzerland.

process has sometimes been rather quick and sometimes slower, when there were political difficulties in the adopting of proper policy measures. The point to emphasize about all these cases of imbalance is that one had no impression at the time that the exchange rate was out of line and that, in fact, adequate adjustment was made without a change in the exchange rate. Analytically, at least, they were not difficult situations.

However, over these 20 years there were some imbalances that clearly required a change in the exchange rate; in other words, there was a fundamental disequilibrium. As a general proposition, I believe it is not wise to conclude too quickly that a given imbalance involves fundamental disequilibrium; it is desirable to wait until the evidence is rather conclusive. This is particularly so when there is excess domestic demand, because it may be difficult to judge the corrective impact on the balance of payments of suppressing the excess demand.

I recall, for example, that when Germany got into difficulties in 1950 and Italy in 1963, there was some opinion in favor of a devaluation of the currency. However, this was proven to be quite unnecessary once the overheated state of the economy was brought under control; both the German mark and the lira were strong currencies in the years which followed the respective crises. It would certainly have been a mistake to devalue the exchange rate in either case, as the likely consequence would have been a higher level of domestic prices.

There have been other cases where the signs that the exchange rate was out of line became overwhelming. Due to the substantial inflation in France during the war in Algeria, it became clear that the external deficit could not be corrected without a devaluation of the franc. I thought at the time that a change in the rate should have been incorporated in the stabilization program initiated at the end of 1957; however, the Government was not prepared to take this step at that time and it was not until the end of 1958 that the currency was devalued and the franc stabilized. In retrospect I am not sure now that waiting a year was a mistake, because by that time the fiscal and monetary restraints of the stabilization program had had a chance to cool off the domestic boom. Hence, when the devaluation came, it quickly yielded good adjustment results.

Similarly, in the case of the Spanish stabilization program of 1959, it was evident that a substantial change in the exchange rate would be needed to make the balance of payments viable. This step was taken at the same time as fiscal and monetary restraints were imposed and, as the domestic restraints were rigidly held for a period of six months, the adjustment process implicit in the devaluation worked like a charm.

An interesting case of imbalance on the surplus side was the German mark in the 1950s. At that time the balance-of-payments deficit of the United States was rather small so that the German surplus was considered to be exerting significant pressure on other European countries. You will remember that, after the exchange rate had been fixed at the time of the currency reform, there was a further devaluation in 1949. Whether this was appropriate is an open question, but in any case it became quite clear that the German mark was undervalued as the productive potential of the economy was restored in subsequent years. The revaluation of the German mark was seriously considered in 1957, which caused some disturbance in exchange markets, but no action was taken. You will remember, however, that the currency was revalued in 1961. I believe it is generally agreed that earlier action would have been in the interests of monetary stability domestically and a contribution to the international adjustment process.

The point I have been trying to make in citing these cases is the following: most countries have experienced significant external imbalance at one time or another in the past 20 years; as an exercise in applied economics it has generally not been very difficult to analyze the situation and to decide on the corrective measures required to make the adjustment mechanism work — including a judgment about the appropriateness of the rate of exchange. The two exceptions have been the United Kingdom and the United States where there have been both analytical and operational difficulties.

Sterling Crises

As you know, sterling was subject to a series of exchange crises over the years since the devaluation of 1949 and eventually it was devalued again in November 1967. This was a difficult case for two reasons: firstly, it was not easy to say at what point in time there was clear evidence of overvaluation; secondly, it was not easy to know what to do about it. So far as the exchange crises in the 1950s are concerned, there were special circumstances in each instance which made it doubtful that fundamental disequilibrium was involved. In

1952 the special factors were the excess demand generated by a heavy rearmament program and the high prices of raw material imports associated with the Korean war. In 1955, although the balance of payments was again in deficit to some degree, the exchange market was upset by discussions of a proposal for wider bands. In 1957 the balance of payments was actually in surplus when the market was upset mainly because of the rumors of a German mark revaluation. The exchange difficulties in all these instances were rather short-lived and there did not appear to be any necessity to protect the exchange rate by excessive unemployment. Indeed, there was rather some reason to say that the economy was generally under demand pressure.

The next sterling crisis was a rather different matter. After the economy had stagnated for four years, a strong stimulus to expansion was given by the budget of 1959 and several other measures. In not much more than a year a significant external deficit developed and a shift in policy to restraining measures became necessary. It was reasonably clear, therefore, that a situation had been reached in which economic growth comparable to other industrial countries could not be maintained without an external deficit — which is surely indicative of fundamental disequilibrium. Anyone not convinced of the overvaluation of sterling at that time had little reason to miss this judgment when the renewed expansionary policy reflected in the budget of 1963 led to a large external deficit by mid-1964 and then to the exchange crisis later in the year.

But what to do about it? It was highly probable that a simple devaluation exercise would not work. Devaluation could, of course, be made to secure a balanced external position on the flows of transactions arising currently. However, it was almost certain to lead to significant liquidation of foreign-held sterling balances, particularly those in the reserves of sterling-area countries. While such diversification of reserves in sterling might not come all in a rush, it would exert a constant pressure on sterling and make a new fixed exchange rate at least fragile and probably untenable. My own view on the matter was that allowing the rate to float for some time was the most realistic way out of the dilemma.

In the event, sterling was devalued to a new fixed rate in November 1967, and it was not long before the expected drain from the sterling balances was evident. The difficulty was resolved by the second group arrangement through the BIS to provide financial support to the UK authorities against adverse movements of the sterling balances. The United Kingdom on its side gave guarantees on official sterling-area holdings of sterling, and the group of central banks and the BIS gave reasonable assurances of the liquidity at the guaranteed rate of the reserves held in sterling. This imaginative exercise in monetary cooperation has worked very successfully — aided by the fact that policy measures to support the devaluation have themselves been effective. It must be considered a good outcome to a quite difficult problem.

The Dollar Problem

The other really complicated, and controversial, case has been the dollar. The United States has had a balance-of-payments deficit almost continuously since 1950. No economist has contended that the dollar has been continuously in fundamental disequilibrium over this period and there is little agreement on the root causes of the difficulty. To make matters worse, there is no consensus on how equilibrium for the US balance of payments should be defined, in view of the complications arising from the fact that the dollar is the intervention currency and the dynamic reserve currency of the international monetary system.

I have myself defined external equilibrium for the United States in a growing world economy as an upward trend in US gold reserves sufficient to maintain confidence in the convertibility of the dollar in the face of growing reserve holdings of dollars. According to this definition the balance of payments has been in disequilibrium for most of the past 20 years. I believe that several causes are involved in fully explaining this disequilibrium, that sometimes acted together and sometimes had much different quantitative importance.

Firstly, the US external position has at times been affected by adverse cyclical movements at home and abroad, as for example in the years 1958-59.

Secondly, there has been an adverse effect at times from domestic excess demand, particularly evident during the period of the Vietnam war.

Thirdly, it is fair to say that the United States did not take effective measures to correct the external deficit, apart from the imposition of direct controls on the outflow of capital. In particular, monetary policy was generally conducted as if the United States were a closed economy, and the differential between domestic and foreign interest rates was sufficiently wide at times to induce large outflows of funds. It was argued in the early 1960s that a higher priority in monetary policy on the external situation would not be effective, but the case was never convincing and the opposite has since been demonstrated.

Fourthly, a basic factor in the losses of gold reserves over the entire period has been the shortage of new gold available to the monetary system. In effect, the demand for gold by foreign monetary authorities in a surplus position was larger than could be supplied by new gold availabilities. The tendency was for the shortage to be made up by net purchases from the United States. It seems to be more correct in these circumstances to say that gold and the system were in fundamental disequilibrium, rather than that the dollar itself was in fundamental disequilibrium. In any case, the remedy available to the United States was to negotiate a change in the gold parity of the dollar with the IMF. This seems to me to be the adjustment process called for in the Bretton Woods system. But, for what I believe to be political considerations, the United States has not chosen this course.

The adherence to the existing gold parity of the dollar in the face of the growing shortage of gold has been leading to fundamental changes in the Bretton Woods system — at times threatening its breakdown. There has been a growth of direct controls by both deficit and surplus countries. In addition, gold reserves have tended to freeze up due to the uncertainty surrounding the price of gold. Moreover, without an adequate inflow of new gold into the system, the free growth of dollar reserves has been inhibited so that the growth of reserves has depended largely upon special credit transactions among monetary authorities. Finally, in the absence of a semi-autonomous growth of gold and dollar reserves, pressures on exchange rates have become more and more frequent and several major changes in rates have taken place. I believe that a solution to the gold problem is required as a foundation for an effective adjustment mechanism, and I find it difficult to imagine that the introduction of SDRs alone will solve the problem.

GOTTFRIED HABERLER

Speaking as the fourth member of this panel presents certain problems, not only of time but also of space. The two sides of the spectrum have been firmly occupied by Milton F. and Milton G., and Dick Caves has covered much of the middle ground in his speech. So I will have to find a few gaps, but I will also have to leave a little bit of space for the next speaker.

I shall follow Milton G. in discussing primarily the problem of the financially "disciplined" countries — that is, roughly speaking, the industrial world. As far as the undisciplined countries — most of the less developed countries — are concerned, I think the balance-of-payments problem is quite simple and intellectually (although not politically) much easier than for the developed countries. Milton G. said he didn't know what to do about them, but I think he did not really mean that. What these countries have got to do is to adjust their exchange rates — and the more quickly and frequently the better. The most inflationary countries — like Chile and Brazil — have found out that they must depreciate their currencies more or less automatically every two or three weeks. This surely is not an ideal situation, but if prices rise 30 percent a year or more, there is practically no other way out than to depreciate the currency at short intervals — that is, to introduce a sort of trotting peg. That is what Brazil, Colombia, Chile have been doing in recent years and expert observers, including foreign businessmen doing business in those countries, agree that the trotting peg is a great improvement over the system formerly in use under which rates were kept nominally stable by means of an intricate system of controls for half a year or longer and then changed with a bang by a large amount.

Turning now to the "disciplined" countries, the trouble is that they are not equally disciplined. And experience seems to show that small differences in financial discipline, resulting in comparatively slight differences in the rate of inflation, can have a profound influence on the balance of payments. This is the consequence of the

*The author has discussed the problems in greater detail in his pamphlet *Money in the International Economy*, 2nd edition, Harvard University Press, 1969.

Mr. Haberler is Galen L. Stone Professor of International Trade, Harvard University, Cambridge, Massachusetts.

fact, emphasized by Dick Caves, that the economic interconnected-ness and integration of the developed countries, especially but by no means exclusively of the members of EEC and EFTA, have made great progress; despite existing barriers and restrictions, trade and capital flows have grown by leaps and bounds and have become very responsive to price and interest differentials.

I shall follow Milton F.'s example and confine myself to the adjustment problem in the strict sense and not discuss what economists call the "confidence" and "liquidity" problem. The adjustment mechanism is clearly of paramount importance. If balance-of-payments disequilibria are not speedily eliminated either by the automatic forces of the market or by discretionary policy measures, huge amounts of international reserves (liquidity) may be needed and confidence crises are bound to occur from time to time. On the other hand, the more quickly and efficiently the adjustment mechanism works, the shorter the spells of imbalance, the less liquidity is needed to tide countries over periods of deficit.

Primacy of Adjustment Problems

The primacy of adjustment over liquidity has been officially recognized in the SDR agreement. According to Article XXIV of the amended IMF Charter, the SDR's are to be activated if there is "the likelihood of a better working of the adjustment process in the future."[1]

As you all know, the SDR scheme has actually been "activated" at the recent IMF annual meeting and the first allocations will be made in the near future. I am not sure that we really can assume that the mechanism will work better from now on. But at least the priority of the adjustment problem has been officially recognized.

Let me now briefly describe the adjustment mechanism and the principles of adjustment policies under fixed exchanges.

Adjustment Policies under Fixed Exchanges

I follow the example of previous speakers and distinguish between

---

[1] The language of the Charter is as follows: "The first decision to allocate special drawing rights shall take into account, as special considerations, a collective judgment that there is a global need to supplement reserves, and the attainment of a better balance of payments equilibrium, as well as the likelihood of a better working of the adjustment process in the future." Article XXIV, Section I(b) of the *Articles of Agreement of the International Monetary Fund* as modified in 1968.

monetary and real changes. Balance-of-payments disequilibria can be caused by real or monetary factors. A deficit — and the corresponding surplus — may be the consequence of autonomous inflation, more precisely one country autonomously inflating faster than others. (This is a quite general statement, if we regard deflation as negative inflation, keeping in mind that cases of real deflation have hardly occurred during the postwar years.) "Autonomous" means not induced by the state of the balance of payments, but by domestic forces or dictated by domestic considerations. But a deficit can also be the consequence of a "real" change, that is, by what economists call "a shift in international demand" for any reason whatever. In theory it is easy to make this distinction notwithstanding the possibility of mixed cases.

Offhand, I would say that monetary disturbances — differences in the rate of inflation — are a more important cause of imbalances than real disturbances, shifts in international demand. If prices in many less developed countries rise by 20 percent or more the case is clear. But in the "disciplined" countries it is perhaps not quite so clear that monetary causes account for most imbalances.

Let me give an example. Many of you have probably seen or read about an important recent paper by Professor Hendrik Houthakker. (H.S. Houthakker and S.P. Magee, "Income and Prices Elasticities in World Trade," *Review of Economics and Statistics,* May 1969.) The authors try to show that the income elasticities of demand for the exports of different industrial countries are substantially different. The two extremes are Japan and Great Britain with the United States in the middle. World demand for Japan's exports is supposed to be very elastic with respect to income, while world demand for British exports is inelastic. As a consequence, when world income grows, demand for British exports rises more slowly than demand for Japanese exports. This would be a non-monetary factor influencing the balance of payments of the two countries. I am not sure that Houthakker's statistical methods enable him to discriminate sharply between income elasticities and other factors influencing the balance of payments of different countries. I mentioned it only as an example of non-monetary, in this case a pervasive "structural," disturbance. It is easy to think of many other real changes that may put the payments balance of some countries in the red and that of others in the black.

In practice, it may often be very difficult to decide whether a particular imbalance has in the last resort been due primarily to monetary or to non-monetary factors, or a mixture of the two. But I submit that this is not a serious handicap for the policymaker. For it is not true, contrary to what is often said, that a different adjustment mechanism and policy is required according to whether the imbalance is due to differential inflation (monetary cause) or a shift in international demand (real cause).[2]

It is not difficult to show how the adjustment mechanism should work and what financial policies should be pursued under fixed exchanges to assure smooth adjustment, without imposing direct controls, irrespective of what the deeper causes of the existing fundamental disequilibrium are. ("Fundamental" we call an imbalance that is so large and persistent that mere financing is no longer possible.)

As Caves has pointed out, there are automatic forces of adjustment at work which tend to reduce an imbalance which has arisen for any reason whatever. I need not describe them again. Suffice it to say that they work today as they did in the past under the regime of the gold standard.

It is sometimes claimed that in order to bring about balance-of-payments adjustment monetary policy should simply refrain from counteracting or offsetting the automatic forces; these would, if left alone, restore equilibrium.

Conflict between Domestic and Balance-of-Payments Objectives

This advice is, however, not easy to translate into quantitative rules for monetary policy and difficult to carry out because monetary policy has important domestic objectives, maintenance of employment, growth, etc. which may be in conflict with the requirements of balance-of-payments adjustment.

[2]One finds frequently the following formulation: If an imbalance is due to "excessive demand" the proper corrective measure is elimination of the excess by monetary retrenchment (disinflation). But if the imbalance is due to a "cost disparity" a change in the exchange rate is indicated.

However, this theory overlooks that no sharp distinction can be made between the two types of causes, for the simple fact that "excessive demand" in the sense of "excessive inflation" (i.e. compared with abroad) will quickly bring about "cost disparities." It is entirely a matter of degree and the proposed rule amounts to saying that mild imbalances should be dealt with by disinflation while serious ones require a change in the exchange rate. This is sensible enough, but does not take us any farther than the familiar rule that only "fundamental" disequilibria justify exchange rate changes. The formula in question does *not* provide criteria for distinguishing fundamental from non-fundamental disequilibria.

But "letting free play for the automatic forces of adjustment" surely implies that monetary policy should assume a somewhat restrictionist stance. The following general rule would seem to cover the whole problem, letting automatic forces work as well as discretionary policies: In order to eliminate balance-of-payments disequilibria, deficit countries should restrict their monetary growth and surplus countries should stimulate it somewhat. If wages and prices were flexible, this prescription could be carried out without seriously endangering employment. Even if wages are quite rigid downward, as is actually the case in most countries, adjustment could still work without causing much unemployment, at least in progressive economies where labor productivity (output per man) rises. All that would be needed in deficit countries is that for a certain period, say a year or two, money wages be kept stable by sufficiently tight money, or at least be allowed to rise only a little less than average productivity rises. Then money costs and prices in the deficit countries would gradually fall and this would tend to restore international balance, provided the surplus countries do their part by letting wages rise a little faster than productivity so that their money costs and prices go up.

Thus, ideally, an adjustment is possible that does not impose undue deflation and unemployment on the deficit countries nor undue inflation on the surplus countries nor impart an inflationary bias on the world as a whole. (I do not call it deflation if prices fall slowly because *money* wages, on the average, rise less than labor productivity. Note that this would *not* imply a lag in *real* wages.) True, this process may take some time. But if it could be counted upon to work in the end, international reserves (liquidity) could be provided to finance the deficit during the interval.

Unfortunately, things often don't work out that way. Even the just mentioned modest minimum requirement of smooth adjustment seems to be impossible of achievement in many countries. There is a well-nigh irresistible wage push in some countries and demand-pull inflation of varying intensity is going on almost everywhere.

The Need for Guidance by Domestic Objectives

The basic difficulty, as I see it, is that everywhere monetary and fiscal policy is, and in the opinion of most economists should be, guided primarily by domestic objectives — full employment, growth, price stability, etc. This was different during the gold standard period when exchange stability and gold convertibility were the overriding considerations. Furthermore, priorities which different countries put on different policy objectives — especially on employment and growth as against price stability — are not the same. Some — the Germans for example — are more concerned with inflation, others, e.g. the British, with employment. Equally important, the intensity of the wage push is different in different countries — Germany and Great Britain offer an illuminating contrast.

The consequence is that the adjustment mechanism without changes in exchange rates and without controls could only work by means of differential inflation, the surplus countries always inflating more than the deficit countries, imparting a strong inflationary bias on the world economy. This is, however, not acceptable for the surplus countries. And in fact during the postwar period there have been a large number of exchange rate changes, a long string of currency depreciations and a few appreciations — three to be exact. The Bretton Woods agreement did not, in fact, provide the world with a system of fixed and stable exchanges.

Smoother Exchange Adjustment Needed

There is almost general agreement now that the current system of infrequent, large changes of exchange rates, the so-called "adjustable peg" system, is unsatisfactory, because it leads necessarily to large capital flows before and after each depreciation or appreciation. As time goes on, more and more people catch on to the pattern and the speculative flows tend to become larger from one crisis to the next.

Most experts, even many who only a few years ago were firm supporters of the system of fixed exchanges, have reached the conclusion that a smoother method of exchange rate adjustment must be found. I need not discuss in detail the different methods of exchange flexibility which have been proposed — unlimited and limited flexibility, crawling peg, upward crawling peg, wider band or a combination of the two, automatic adjustment of rates by formula or discretionary changes; this will be done in some of the other sessions of the conference.

I must confine myself to two final remarks: First, greater flexibility of rates does not mean that every currency in the world will fluctuate against every other. Many small countries will prefer to peg their currencies to that of a large country and groups of countries may well join in fixed currency blocs.

Second, the dollar is in a special position, because it is the world's foremost international reserve currency, intervention currency for foreign central banks, and private investment and transactions currency. It is now fairly generally recognized that as things are the United States could not unilaterally depreciate the dollar or let it float, even if it wanted to. The reason is that if the United States did declare a devaluation of the dollar in terms of gold of, say, 10 percent, practically all other countries, with the only exception of two or three hard currency countries,[3] would go along. Similarly, if the United States suspended gold payments and declared that it would let the dollar float, most other countries would continue to peg their currencies to the dollar.

But what about flexibility? How can it be attained under these circumstances? The answer is that the decision to introduce flexibility has to be left to other countries. If any country feels that pegging its currency to the dollar exposes it to undue inflationary (or deflationary) pressures, that the United States is "exporting inflation" (or deflation) as the phrase goes, it should let its currency float or crawl (up or down according to the circumstances). This does, of course, not mean that the United States should not discuss these problems with others in the IMF, OECD or in the Group of Ten. But the final decision to introduce flexibility will have to be made by others. This decision will, however, be influenced, in the long run probably decisively, by U.S. domestic monetary policy. If we check inflation and give the dollar again a stable purchasing power, we provide the world with a dependable and desirable reserve medium. If, on the other hand, the erosion of the dollar's purchasing power continues, we inflict losses on the holders of dollars, the usefulness of the dollar as an international reserve is impaired and the dollar's status as a reserve, intervention and transactions currency is undermined, although it seems to take a good deal of prolonged inflation to bring that about. It is impossible to foresee exactly what this course of events would eventually lead to. But we can be sure that it would spell troubles, recriminations and instability. Let us hope that inflation will be checked so that we need not find out.

---

[3] Now, after the large upvaluation of the German mark, there would probably be no exception at all, save perhaps the Russian ruble or the Swiss franc.

PANEL

ROBERT SOLOMON

There is an advantage in being the last speaker on a panel; in contrast to the first speaker, the last speaker has the option whether or not to ignore what other speakers have said. I had written some notes for myself, and I fully expected that every one of my points would have been covered by at least one or more of the other speakers. Many of them have, but I am pleased to discover that there are still one or two things I can say that have not yet been said this morning. I shall try to run very lightly over those items on which I would simply be repeating what has been said before, at the same time not impinging on what comes later in the program.

Need for Non-Disruptive Adjustment

In a program with the title of this one, it is useful to start with the question, why do we care about the adjustment process in the first place? Why is it important? I think that the point Milton Friedman made is the right one — that adjustment will occur in any event, primarily because deficit countries can't go on forever in deficit, and they will have to take some action to eliminate the deficit. It is desirable that the actions they take and how they take them not be disruptive to themselves or to their trading partners. Furthermore, it is important that the process of adjustment be consistent with optimum resource allocation, rather than harmful to resource allocation. It is desirable in particular that adjustment be carried out with a minimum of controls — at least those controls that are harmful to resource allocation. All of that is to state what is fairly obvious.

Importance of When and How

This concern about the adjustment process which, as several speakers have said, has come very much to the fore, has, of course, led to discussion about exchange rates. Let me more or less agree with Milton that the issue is not one of fixed versus flexible exchange

Mr. Solomon is Adviser to the Board, Board of Governors of the Federal Reserve System, Washington, D.C.

rates. In my own view, Milton may have exaggerated a little bit the extent to which exchange rate adjustment has been used in the post-war period. I think he has managed to cover almost every industrial country except the U.S. and Japan by including the 1949 set of devaluations which were a sort of "one-shot" adjustment to what had happened during the war. Be that as it may, the idea that exchange rates should remain really fixed among developed countries was somewhat prevalent in the 1950's and early in the 1960's. That view has, I think, been dissipated in recent years and perhaps the best evidence I can use, and the quickest way to say it, is to note a very recent paper by Bob Roosa who, I think it is not unfair to say, had leanings toward the view that rates should remain fixed. In a recent paper, he very eloquently explains why that view was appropriate earlier in the sixties and is not appropriate today. So it is not a question of fixed rates versus flexible rates. The real issue is not *should* exchange rates be changed but *when* and *how* should they be adjusted when they need to be adjusted.

The reasons have been stated very often why the so-called adjustable peg system has not been working well. I won't go over those reasons, but the words "politics," "prestige" and so on get mentioned in that sort of explanation.

Another point about the present adjustable peg system, and an important point, is that when countries do adjust their rates in the discrete, occasional way that is regarded as the hallmark of the present adjustable peg system, there is a tendency for those who devalue to devalue excessively and when an occasional revaluation does occur, it tends to be deficient. That, I would say, is a shortcoming of the system as it has worked up to now.

Now what to do about all this? I am not going to try to impinge on what comes later in the program. One can certainly imagine that without any changes in the Articles of Agreement there could somehow be brought about a change in atmosphere — a change in the behavior of governments — so that the existing par value system would be used for smoother, less disruptive exchange rate adjustment than in the past. This is quite conceivable. To state the case more extremely, one can imagine that countries would somehow be induced to begin to regard small changes in exchange rates, even discrete discretionary ones, as a sort of technical adjustment of an economic policy instrument rather than a major political decision. I might shock both the central bankers and the noncentral bankers here if I made an analogy between small changes in the discount rate

— or bank rate — on the one hand and small changes in the exchange rate on the other. Changes in the discount rate are more or less outside the political sphere. They are regarded as technical adjustments. It is conceivable that a change in attitude toward exchange rates could be brought about whereby one would begin to think of small changes in exchange rates in somewhat the same way one thinks of small changes in central bank discount rates.

Beyond this, there is a spectrum of proposals for greater exchange rate flexibility running all the way from full flexibility to full discretion. And these proposals tend to shade into each other. One of the well-known proposals is the so-called gliding parity in which the parity is established each quarter or so on the basis of an average of market rates in the past. Even such an automatic system would presumably require some sort of agreement or rules of the game on intervention in the exchange market by monetary authorities. It is unlikely, as Milton Friedman and others have said, that central banks would completely eschew their prerogative to intervene. There would be some discretion even in such a system. That system shades into a system of discretionary crawling pegs in which there would be presumptive rules to guide discretionary changes, along the lines of suggestions by Bob Triffin and others. My main purpose here is not to go into the details of these various proposals but to indicate that they aren't all terribly far away from each other.

Need for Bias Toward Revaluation

My next to last point is that, as we think about various devices for improving the adjustment mechanism, there is much to be said for trying to inject into the exchange rate system a bias toward revaluation. I have already noted that the system now contains a bias toward devaluation. This is so in two senses: first, devaluations occur much more frequently than revaluations; second, devaluations tend to be much larger than revaluations because, as I said earlier, those who devalue prefer to overshoot the mark, while those who revalue have every reason from their point of view to undershoot the mark. I think there now exists a convergence of interests in the direction of biasing the system toward revaluation. We have heard proposals from some European officials in favor of an upward crawling peg, which is one way of injecting a bias toward revaluation. They feel that anti-inflationary discipline would be stronger if it were somehow more difficult for countries to devalue than to revalue — more difficult in the sense of the procedures required in the Fund. Their feeling is that if it were more difficult to devalue than to revalue, then perhaps domestic anti-inflationary policies would be stronger than otherwise. Countries would not feel that they could just devalue and therefore offset the effects of inflationary domestic policies. There is another reason why some European officials have a preference toward a system with a bias toward revaluation; they feel that it is a way for countries who don't inflate to protect themselves from the inflation of their trade partners. Those two related reasons converge with the interest of the United States in the system. Given what Professor Haberler has said — that the United States cannot change its exchange rate by its own initiative — it is in the interest of the United States that there not be excessive devaluations against the dollar over time. Since the bias now exists toward devaluation as against revaluation, there is something to be said if we try to change the system by offsetting that with a bias in the other direction.

My final and very brief point is really a reaction to Milton Friedman. I can't resist disagreeing with him on the relevance of SDR's to the adjustment process. I was presumptuous enough to send to the members of this group a paper which I happened to give last week — in Chicago, of all places — which tries to make the case — *I* think with great success — that a steady increase in reserves is a necessary though not a sufficient condition for an effective working of the balance-of-payments adjustment process.

Stabilizing the Present International Payments System

SIR MAURICE H. PARSONS

In the general discussion of the international adjustment process at the present conference, it has fallen to me to discuss the ways and means of stabilising the present system. I shall have something to say later about various approaches which either already exist or have been proposed as innovations to help render the international monetary system more stable than it is. But before considering solutions to the alleged problem, it is, I think, worth spending a little time analysing the nature of the problem itself and forming a judgment as to how serious it in fact is. How deficient has the international adjustment mechanism actually been?

Test of a Successful Exchange System

We might perhaps begin by asking what would be the tests of an ideal or, at least, a generally successful adjustment process. I should like to suggest three.

First, no individual country's external surpluses or deficits should be too large or too prolonged. Secondly, the correction of such surpluses and deficits as do occur should be achieved in ways which do not impose either on individual countries or on the world as a whole, unacceptable inflation or deflation or physical restrictions on trade and payments. Thirdly, the maximum sustainable expansion of trade and activity in both individual economies and in the world as a whole should be facilitated.

Of course, as I have stated them these tests would need to be more explicit: one would have to define — or reach international agreement upon — what was the precise meaning of the expressions "too large," "too prolonged," and "unacceptable." There will always be room for argument and for legitimate differences of opinion on these matters, for what is involved is the achievement of a number of different aims many of which may conflict, and to which different

Sir Parsons is Deputy Governor, Bank of England, London, England.

people and different countries can attach varying degrees of importance. However, I think it is useful to bear these general criteria in mind, even if they cannot be turned into a precise yardstick, when discussing the alleged shortcomings of the international adjustment process or the possibilities of improving it.

Perhaps the most important characteristic of the existing international adjustment process is that it is in no way automatic or mechanical in its working. One can conceive, at least in theory, of systems which would involve an automatic mechanism. For example, under a fully rigorous classical gold standard system in which all currencies were immutably related to gold, and gold formed the basis of an immutable relationship to all credit creation, both domestic and international, there would presumably be no problem of prolonged external imbalances.

It could, however, produce violent domestic inflations and deflations in securing this external adjustment so that while my first criterion might be met, my second certainly would not. Another theoretical possibility might be to solve the problem of international adjustment by having either no foreign trade sector at all, or one which was totally regulated in all aspects – siege economies with some international barter. Such an arrangement might meet my first and second criteria but certainly not my third. The costs in wealth and welfare would obviously be large.

Few knowledgeable people in the western world would, I think, advocate either of these extreme approaches to the adjustment problem. But there is a third theoretical possibility – a regime of completely flexible exchange rates – which, though I believe it would be equally disastrous, does, I am afraid, command support in some quarters.

Theoretically, at least, totally flexible rates could eliminate surpluses and deficits altogether: but at enormous cost. We should have to expect large fluctuations in exchange rates as capital flows and speculative movements of all kinds would be superimposed on whatever misalignments might emerge on current account. There would be serious danger of cumulative movements: once a currency began to float downwards, the speculative pressures on the rate, the increase in costs – particularly in countries which are heavily dependent on imports for food and raw materials – and the inflationary expectations engendered would all tend to work through to export prices and to domestic consumer spending, continually eroding whatever competitive edge had previously been attained and adding to the balance-of-payments problems.

Moreover, a general system of individually floating rates truly determined only by market forces is something of a pipe dream. Once the present system of fixed parities had been abandoned political pressures to manipulate the exchange rate, whether in the interests of such worthy causes as price stability or stable levels of employment or for less worthy motives, would become irresistible. Such a system would therefore tend to elevate the forces of economic nationalism and reduce the international co-operation which has been a major element in the growth of the world economy over the last two decades. We should see competitive depreciations, and the raising of tariff and other barriers by one country after another, just as happened in the 1930s.

I think we can also take it for granted that international trade would be adversely affected if traders were constantly faced by exchange rate risks which it would be quite impracticable to offset by cheap forward cover. The experience of Canada in the 1950s is sometimes quoted to suggest that fears of floating rates are exaggerated. But the reason for the Canadian float was basically unique in that it was introduced in order to offset the inflationary impact of the massive inflow of capital from the United States. It is one thing for a single country to float in a context of generally fixed rates, but it is quite another matter to contemplate all the large trading nations, including the reserve currency centres, floating against one another. Moreover, even in the Canadian case the floating rate raised serious problems which led to the resumption of a fixed rate.

The Bretton Woods System as a Compromise

The Bretton Woods system is a compromise arrangement between all these various theoretical extremes. It aims to provide a framework in which trade and payments can be very considerably liberalised, in which orderly economic relationships and a high measure of economic co-operation can flourish, at the same time allowing a good deal of internal sovereignty to each country in determining its domestic economic policies. In this system there is no *automatic* mechanism for adjustment. When, in the pursuit of domestic aims, a country runs into external imbalance — either surplus or deficit — a wide variety of responses are open to it. It can finance the deficit or surplus by drawing down or running up reserves, or by borrowing from or lending abroad. It can act to depress or expand the level of internal activity, and it can impose or liberalise controls on various sectors of its balance of payments — particularly capital movements. Another alternative is for it to make a change down or up in its exchange rate parity.

In principle, with full knowledge of the facts and with a clear idea of relative priorities, the authorities in any given country should be able to choose a set of policies which adjusts the external position with least damage or most benefit to internal aims. A country with an excess level of domestic activity and an external deficit can deflate; although the impact of inflation on domestic costs may lead to the necessity to devalue and this will add to the problems of offsetting inflation. A country with too low a level of domestic activity combined with an external deficit may also be diagnosed to have an over-valued currency and can therefore devalue; a country merely suffering a temporary or seasonal deficit should be able to finance it.

In practice, of course, knowledge of the situation is far from perfect and judgment about trends and future possibilities highly uncertain, so that there can be much argument as to what is the appropriate policy in any country at any time. Because of this, the adjustment mechanism is far from automatic and the likelihood arises of incompatible objectives in different countries and harmful interactions between countries. It is quite possible that under the present system the adjustment process might in practice fail to meet one or more of the three criteria I listed earlier.

Let us look briefly at recent experience and see what our judgment on the system should be. We may take as the relevant period the decade since the major trading countries of the world achieved full external convertibility in 1958. Up to that date the world could probably be described as still in a state of prolonged post-war transition, and not fully operating the true Bretton Woods system.

For reasons which I shall come back to, I shall first leave the United Kingdom and the United States to one side. If we then examine the experience of the other major countries of the world, we have, I think, very striking evidence of an active and effective adjustment mechanism at work. First we have an unprecedented expansion in world trade and activity: 8½ percent per annum increase in trade and 6 percent increase in industrial production.

Associated with this, there has been a strong though not unbroken general trend towards tariff reduction and liberalisation of current and capital payments.

This was not achieved without producing external strains and imbalances. On the contrary, all major countries in the world experienced substantial movements into both surplus and deficit. All of them at different times during the 10 years had to undertake policies to correct their external position. A large variety of weapons was used, and in a number of cases there were short-term and unwelcome consequences on national activity or welfare. But these were generally short-lived, and the underlying trend continued for all of them to be satisfactory.

Perhaps a few examples are worth quoting. Germany, often considered to be an almost permanent structural creditor, experienced two substantial periods of deficit in the past decade: for seven quarters, in 1961/62, a total deficit of $1.5 billion, and for nine quarters, in 1964/66, a deficit of $2.7 billion. This latter deficit resulted primarily from domestic overheating: deflationary action was taken and the deficit was turned into a substantial surplus which continued until this year. In 1969, as is not always realised, the Germans have again been running a moderate deficit on current and long-term capital account combined, as a result of determined efforts to offset their large current account surplus with an even larger capital outflow.

The Italian economy became overheated in the early 1960s, causing a loss of confidence and a deficit of nearly $2 billion over an 18-month period in 1962/64. This was cured by deflationary domestic action which led to fairly rapid correction of the position and was soon followed by an export boom and substantial surplus.

Japan experienced three external deficits amounting to $1.3 billion in 1961/62, $1 billion in 1963/64, and $1.4 billion in 1967/68. Each of these was related to excessive domestic activity, each was tackled by domestic restraint and each was succeeded by a period of surplus. With the partial exception of Italy, where demand may be said to have remained somewhat deficient for rather too long after the deflationary action in 1964, all these countries experienced only relatively small and short-lived setbacks in the rate of increase of their domestic activity. Other similar, if less dramatic, examples of movements from surplus to deficit and back again could be quoted from many other countries in the world.

I would maintain, therefore, that the alleged difficulties of the present system have centred very much on our two countries, to a brief discussion of which I now turn.

The U.K. Experience

There is no question, I am afraid, but that the United Kingdom record has been unsatisfactory. In the 1950s our external position was broadly in balance, current account surpluses being normally roughly offset by capital account deficits, but because of the inadequate level of our external reserves in relation to our short-term liabilities, we should have been running surpluses. In the 1960s the position steadily deteriorated with current account surpluses being replaced by increasingly large deficits and the capital account deficits only being reduced by severe, and in the long run damaging, exchange controls. In the five years 1964/68 we had a cumulative deficit on long-term current and capital account of $5.6 billion. At last, after many delays and disappointments, and following a long series of official actions – including of course the devaluation of sterling in November 1967 – the United Kingdom appears to have moved out of deficit; and I think there are grounds for cautious optimism that the position will continue to improve.

However, it is clear that the United Kingdom has experienced a deficit that could be called too large and too prolonged on anybody's definitions. There have doubtless been many reasons for this. With her persistent trends of low productivity increase, high wage increases and low proportion of G.N.P. saved and invested, the United Kingdom undoubtedly has had, and continues to have, major structural deficiencies as a competitive productive economy. These deficiencies have considerably complicated the management of the U.K. balance of payments. However, I think there has been another factor operating in the case of the United Kingdom which does not arise from the other countries already discussed: the international status of sterling.

I do not want to be misunderstood. I do not believe that sterling's role as a reserve and trading currency has itself been a factor in producing our deficits. On the contrary, I believe that the trading role is highly profitable and beneficial to the United Kingdom. My point is rather that the ramifications of the widespread holding and use of sterling throughout the world are so far-reaching that an alteration in its value would have such dangers for liquidity, for orderly trade, and for international confidence that there is a natural tendency for the rest of the world to give the United Kingdom the benefit of the doubt and provide financial support for the sterling exchange rate in greater quantities and for longer than would be the case for other currencies.

The chickens came home to roost at last. In the end it was impossible to avoid a devaluation of sterling, and this became widely recognised both at home and abroad. In the end we have, as I have indicated, finally moved out of deficit and are, I hope, on our way to a period of sustained and substantial external surplus such as will be necessary for us to repay our external debt. This process has taken too long. But the reason has been, I suggest, not because the means for adjustment which other countries have had to hand and have successfully used were not available to the U.K. authorities, but rather that there were special factors inhibiting their early use by the United Kingdom.

The U.S. Experience

The U.S. external deficit has certainly been large and prolonged on any definition. Indeed, running at an average of $2.4 billion per year for 10 years it dwarfs any other imbalance in the system. The very fact, however, that it has been so long and so persistent suggests that it has differed in kind from the imbalances of other countries, including the United Kingdom. In the first place, for most of the period, though admittedly there has been a deterioration recently, the United States has run a massive surplus on current account which has been more than offset by capital transfers. Secondly, in earlier years, the deficit and the externally held dollars it generated were strongly welcomed by the rest of the world because they made a very useful contribution to the growth of international liquidity. Thirdly, under the Bretton Woods system the United States has a unique role which makes it almost impossible directly to change its exchange rate vis-à-vis other currencies. It has always been able to change the value of the dollar in relation to gold, of course, but such action, had it been taken, would not have constituted a devaluation or revaluation of the dollar in the normal sense because of the strong probability that all other currencies would change their gold values too to the same degree. Thus one of the major weapons at the disposal of other countries for the implementation of the adjustment process has not been available to the United States.

For most of the period the existence of the U.S. deficit has indeed played an important part in facilitating that relative ease of adjustment among other major countries of which I spoke earlier. It has to a large extent been a reflection of the rest of the world's liquidity needs.

Recently, however, matters have changed. Not merely has the willingness to accumulate further dollars deteriorated, but the nature of the U.S. deficit has altered. Inflationary pressures have developed in the United States, whose record until 1965 was very much better than the average, and the current account surplus has virtually disappeared. There is therefore at present a need for contractionary measures by the U.S. authorities on both internal and external grounds and such measures, both monetary and fiscal, are being taken. For some time it was difficult to discern much effect from the Administration's restrictive policies, but the rate of expansion of the U.S. economy is now being significantly moderated, and, in due course, though after a necessary time-lag, the rate of price inflation will also slow down. This together with the beneficial effects of the first issue of S.D.R.s on the rest of the world's demand for U.S. goods and services, should mean a considerable improvement in the U.S. current balance of payments. It is difficult, however, to predict how far the deficit will be reduced and indeed one is by no means enthusiastic that it should change to a surplus given the need of the rest of the world for dollars. Some degree of permanent U.S. deficit — much smaller than of late — could well be an element in a stable pattern of international payments.

Possible Improvements and Stabilisation for the System

It will be clear from my remarks so far that I regard many of the criticisms of the present international monetary system as ill-conceived. The problems and inadequacy of the international adjustment process are often exaggerated. Of course, the system is not perfect, and adjustment takes place less than ideally. Countries normally delay in introducing the appropriate measures. Many mistakes, both of diagnosis and prescription, are made, but I believe that some imperfections are bound to exist in any system. The question remains — can any modifications to the system be introduced which would usefully improve its working?

Some people have been calling lately for a widening of the margins around parity within which currencies must be maintained. Naturally there is nothing sacrosanct about the particular margins of 1 percent either way laid down in the Bretton Woods rules. But I should be strongly opposed to a significant widening (for example to 5 percent either way, as is sometimes proposed) with the idea of trying to improve the adjustment process. Such a widening would immensely complicate international payments, and would appear to me to have the disadvantages of a flexible rate system while the exchange rate varied within the new wider margins, and all of the troubles that are alleged to exist in the present system would remain when the edges of the bands were reached. If a country attempted to achieve a small devaluation simply by letting the exchange rate go to its margin, it would thereupon generate speculative expectations that the parity itself would soon be moved to the point of the market exchange rate, with the possibility therefore of further downward movement. These disadvantages appear to be fairly widely recognised, for I notice that there has been some decline in interest in this particular type of proposed innovation. On the other hand, there continues to be considerable interest in the idea of a so-called "crawling peg" mechanism.

I am sure you are all familiar with the various forms under which this proposal has been put forward, and I understand that others will be analysing their advantages and disadvantages in some detail at this present conference. I shall therefore confine myself here to some rather broad, general remarks.

First, it does not seem to me conceivable that governments could or should sign away their sovereignty, as it were, in the field of the exchange rate by adhering to some form of automatic arrangement whereby, according to some formula, the parity at any one time is determined within narrow limits by developments in the markets or in the external position of the country concerned. Moreover, even if the nations of the world were to agree to let their parities be determined in this automatic way, the problems of regulating perverse intervention by the central banks would I believe be insuperable.

Doubts about the Crawling Peg

The alternative idea, under which countries could by prior announcement make small and gradual movements in their parities, is probably technically feasible, but I have yet to see a number of important questions which it raises satisfactorily answered. First, considering how difficult it is to decide whether a currency is over-valued or under-valued when the degree of possible over- or under-valuation in question is usually 10 percent or more, I cannot see how it would be possible to diagnose a misalignment of 2 percent. But if one waits until the evidence for under- or over-valuation has become relatively strong, it is likely that changing the parity at the rate of, say, 2 percent a year will prove inadequate. This leads me to my second major doubt, which is whether the fact that a currency has begun to "crawl" will not in fact be as likely to increase as to lessen speculative pressure on it, because it would obviously be quite impossible completely to rule out major adjustments. Thirdly, I am doubtful whether a gradual change in the parity will produce the necessary adjustments internally to rectify the external imbalance. It seems to me only too likely, to take a downward crawling example again, that the stimulus given to increased costs and to inflationary expectations generally will, when they work through to exports, negate any competitive advantage originally produced by the downward crawl. Fourthly, I believe that the operation of monetary policy would be complicated by the need to take account externally of the announced steady changes in the value of a currency. More generally, much in the area of international trade and payments flows would be complicated by a system in which a number of important exchange rates were continually moving in one direction or another. Finally, I cannot conceive of how a reserve currency could become a potential crawler. It is my belief, based on some knowledge of the authorities in those countries which have traditionally held sterling as an external reserve, that the fact that the value of their reserve asset was continually liable to change would seriously reduce its attractions for them.

Differences Between Up and Down Flexibility

However, it would be wrong to set one's face against change simply for the sake of adhering to what exists. It may be that some of my doubt can be dispelled by argument and analysis and discussion. In particular, I can see that the possibility for countries to crawl upwards, if they so wished, might not involve all the disadvantages I see in downward crawling and might have some advantages. There seem to me two important differences between permitting more flexibility upwards and permitting more downwards. First, since a country cannot be forced to revalue in the same way as one that is running out of reserves can be forced to devalue, it may be that the markets would accept an upward crawl as the maximum upward movement likely for the particular currency in a way that I have indicated they would very probably not do for a downward crawling currency.

The second difference between upward and downward movement takes us into a much wider area and, in my view, brings us to the heart of the problem. This is that, since in the nature of the Bretton Woods system the United States is virtually powerless to change the parity of the dollar vis-à-vis other currencies, it is important that in the long run the net result of all the various exchange rate alterations by other countries be not too large a movement in one direction or another. In practice, of course, devaluations against the dollar have enormously outweighed revaluations against it. Since there has also been a tendency for prices to rise faster in most of the other countries of the world than in the United States, at least until recently, the overall result of this "devaluation bias" in the system has not been too serious. But it is a potential threat to the system and therefore any device which encourages or makes easier upward changes is worth discussion. (It is, of course, still to be shown that a crawling peg arrangement *would* produce more appropriate revaluations than the present system.)

Problems of International Liquidity

These last considerations lead me back to my main thesis which is that the adjustment process has not always been as inefficient as is often claimed and that it is not at faults in adjustment in *general* that we must look in order to discover the major difficulties under which the international payments system has been labouring. It has been the problem of international liquidity which has been an important source of our difficulties. In the early years of the U.S. deficit, when increases in dollar holdings were desired by the rest of the world, the increased world liquidity produced by the United States facilitated a vigorous and active adjustment process between most countries. In recent years, however, this has no longer been the case, and it has become increasingly clear that we need to look for a new source for extra international liquidity. We have found this, of course, in S.D.R.s which are to come into operation in quite substantial amounts from the beginning of next year.

I regard this as easily the most important step which the international community could have taken towards stabilising the present system and facilitating the adjustment process. With the improved prospects for both the United States and the United Kingdom — the only important countries where the adjustment process has appeared to have been seriously deficient — I think we may see the system functioning much better than it has appeared to do in the past few years; and this may well occur without any of those reforms to the Bretton Woods system which some at the moment believe to be so necessary. Even if the failure of our two countries to achieve adjustment more efficiently may ultimately cause damage to the world economy, the new international liquidity system — if it is functioning effectively — should help to offset the damage.

DISCUSSION

ROBERT TRIFFIN

I will try for a change not to play the part of the prima donna so dear to all of us academics, but to limit myself to six very specific comments directed at the extremely interesting, stimulating, and thoughtful paper of Sir Maurice. I must, of course, by force stress the points of disagreement rather than agreement if I wish to bring any contribution of my own to this discussion and stimulate some exchange of views. But I would like to insist that these points are relatively minor, that Sir Maurice probably does not disagree with most of them, and that I certainly feel in full agreement with the main brunt of his arguments and conclusions.

What I disagree most with, I guess, is the title of his paper, "Stabilizing the Present International Payments System." I don't disagree with "stabilizing," but what I would like to see stabilized is certainly not the present international payments system but a vastly improved one. I suspect that this is also what Sir Maurice has in mind.

The Order of Priorities for an Ideal Adjustment Process

My second point of difference is about the order of priorities in the three tests which he suggests for an ideal adjustment process. I would just about reverse that order. That is to say, I would put first the third test — i.e. to facilitate the maximum sustainable expansion of trade and activity in the world as a whole — and put last, although not neglect, his first point — to avoid too large or too prolonged surpluses or deficits for individual countries. My main reason for reversing Sir Maurice's order of priorities is that large and prolonged surpluses or deficits for an individual country may well be beneficial at times for that country as well as for the world as a whole. He himself gave an example of this in his paper and repeated what Professor Cooper, my colleague at Yale, pointed out many years ago: that the deficits of the United States in the late 1940's and early 1950's were beneficial to all concerned and welcomed by them all. They were beneficial and welcomed, first, as a way to redistribute

Mr. Triffin is Frederick William Beinecke Professor of Economics, Yale University, New Haven, Connecticut.

monetary reserves in a more satisfactory manner, from the excess reserves accumulated by the United States during the war and to replenish the depleted reserve levels of other countries at the end of the war. And they were welcomed also as a way to sustain desirable, feasible, and, on the whole during that period, noninflationary levels of world trade and production which could no longer be fed by adequate accretions to the world stock of monetary gold and could not yet be fed by SDR's, because they did not exist.

External Surplus or Deficit

My third point is a query rather than a disagreement. What is meant by the terms "external surplus" or "external deficit" to which he refers? I suspect from the rest of his paper that Sir Maurice refers very probably to what is called the "basic" deficit or surplus; that is to say, the surplus or deficit on current account and long-term capital account. Or possibly to the Bernstein deficit or surplus on reserve settlements accounts, which includes not only the current account and long-term capital account but also short-term capital movements other than the reserve assets of the domestic and foreign monetary authorities. I myself suggested this latter definition long before Bernstein succeeded in selling it to the U.S. Department of Commerce, and I still think it is a very useful one. Yet recent developments suggest to me that neither can be relied upon as meaningful by itself in isolation from the structure of the balance of payments, from the disaggregated accounts, current account and capital movements. Let me give you a very simple example. The U.S. basic balance or settlement balance could be in perfect equilibrium under two very different conditions. First, we might have a $10 billion current account surplus financed by $10 billion of capital exports. I would not be too dissatisfied with that ideal or that norm, but you could get the same basic equilibrium with a $10 billion deficit on current account financed by a $10 billion of capital imports into the richest and most capitalized country in the world. I would not take those two basic balances as equivalent to one another. I doubt that you would, Sr. Maurice. By the way, we hear a lot today about the fact that in this year the German balance was also in basic equilibrium or even in deficit. I don't take that very seriously either, and I have grave doubts, by the way, about the manner in which we distinguish, in our statistics, long-term and short-term capital movements. I would not be surprised if some so-called short-term working balances were in fact far less volatile than "long-term" capital investments or flings in Wall Street.

No Really Automatic Adjustment Formula

That brings me to my fourth point which, fortunately, is one of agreement rather than disagreement. I share fully Sir Maurice's remark about the naivety of any automatic adjustment formula, whether it be, first, that of a mythical gold standard — a la Rueff — which never existed in history, or secondly, that of an equally utopian floating exchange rate system — à la Milton Friedman — under which central banks would be barred from any intervention whatsoever in the exchange market. There is a great deal of similarity, I think, between the two proposals. No responsible, or even irresponsible, government or monetary authorities will accept tying their hands behind their backs in this way and leaving a policy instrument as powerful as their currency's exchange-rate at the tender mercy of accidental forces and/or currency speculators.

When Exchange Rate Changes Should Be Used

I hardly need to harbor that point in respect to the automatic gold standard — I doubt if there are any defenders of it here — but I might have a few remarks about fully floating exchange rates. I mean fully floating exchange rates without any kind of market intervention by central banks, assuming that this were thinkable. Exchange-rate adjustments, to my mind, cannot be regarded as the universal panacea for all of the major and radically different sources of balance-of-payments disequilibrium. That is to say: first, temporary, reversible disequilibria such as, for instance, due to bad crops or speculative capital movements; secondly, discrepancies in national demand policies, i.e. in relative rates of inflationary or deflationary fiscal or monetary policies. I think that those fiscal and monetary policies should ideally adjust GNP expenditures to the country's productive potential at reasonably full employment. If they don't, you will have continuing surpluses or deficits. And then there is the third source of disequilibrium to which I think the remedy of changes in the exchange rate is applicable and that is disparities in the international price and cost pattern.

Exchange readjustment will often prove the best, or even the only, feasible remedy for the third of these three major sources of disequilibrium, but certainly not for the first two. Temporary disequilibria should be *financed* rather than prematurely and unwisely eliminated by exchange rate changes that would be not readjusting but maladjusting in the long run. Secondly, as far as overspending or underspending is concerned, this should obviously be corrected by appropriate fiscal and monetary action, but not by exchange-rate changes which merely rechannel the resulting disequilibria from the balance of payments to the domestic economy. I have estimated, for instance, that in 1968 the United States spent publicly and privately, for investment or consumption, about $40 billion more than its maximum productive potential. This overflow of expenditures had to find its way both in domestic price increases of 4 percent a year or more and into a substantial shortage of the U.S. current account with relation to any reasonable surplus target that would finance desirable capital exports.[1] We might of course, if other countries allow us to do it, improve our current account by devaluation, but as long as the overspending continued, this would merely accelerate domestic inflationary forces. We would export more and import less, fewer goods would be available, and therefore the domestic absorption of the overspending would simply accelerate price rises that would, as a consequence, create the third type of disequilibrium – under-competitive levels of prices and costs – that would justify that devaluation *ex post*. But as long as overspending continued, inflationary forces would continue also and resurrect a balance-of-payments deficit.

Similarly, the underspending countries, if there are any, could eliminate their consequent surpluses through revaluation of their currency, but only by aggravating domestic deflationary forces. As different from the deficit countries, however, these deflationary forces would translate themselves today into unemployment rather than into wage decreases, and this asymmetry would introduce a devaluation bias in the world exchange-rate system through what my academic friends have dubbed a "ratchet" effect. I refer you again to my previous writing on the subject or shall let you raise questions about it if it is not perfectly clear to you.

Consequences of Floating Rates

In brief, an automatically floating exchange rate system would

[1] See my booklet on *The Fate of the Pound* (Atlantic Institute, Paris, 1969) pp. 22 and 36-37.

bottle up internally the consequences of all mistakes in demand policy. But inflationary mistakes would result in permanent price and wage rises, while deflationary mistakes would result in temporary unemployment rather than in a downward movement of wages. Therefore, there would not be that nice balance that would be tenable in the long run. And, the former mistakes not being offset by the latter, floating currencies would tend over time to float uniformly downward in terms of other currencies or, if all countries were to adopt the system, at least in terms of goods.

These strictures of an automatically floating rate would be compounded under a less automatic system — which is the only one that is realistically conceivable — under which central banks did not abstain permanently from market intervention. First of all such interventions would be very likely to work at cross purposes. There is only one dollar-sterling exchange rate, not two. Who will manage it? The Bank of England or the Federal Reserve System, or both? We know that in the early 1930's the British authorities wanted to see sterling go down in terms of the dollar and the American authorities wanted the dollar to go down in terms of sterling. They could not both have their way, and when they finally realized it they concluded the Tripartite Agreement. I give to my students sometimes the simile with a set of contiguous shower baths, each of them equipped with a faucet that regulates the heat of the water for all of them. I think the bathers would come out and fight. And that is what would happen probably with managed exchange rates in which national authorities were free to manage their rates at cross purposes.

Secondly, and this is a very important point, I think, the market interventions of central banks would not be decided by God or his angels — that is to say, the economists. They would be managed by governments subject to all kinds of pressures from vested interests and lobbies. I refer you to the experience of Latin America, and particularly Argentina, in the 19th century. What happened there was that you had the Cajas de Conversión which would stabilize the exchange rate. When things went bad and the balance of payments was running into heavy deficit they closed the Caja de Conversión and as a result the exchange value of the Argentine peso went down, and the exporters were all very happy. But if later on there was a boom in Argentina as a result of good crops and so on, the exchange rate tended to move up, and immediately all the exporters shrieked that they were getting fewer pesos for their wheat or for their meat and all the economists joined in applauding the re-opening of the

Caja de Conversión. The rate could not be allowed to move up for very long and so you had a succession of downward movements very much like a staircase. This was true in most of the Latin American countries and I am afraid would be true again under such a system. Finally, a system of floating exchange rates would to my mind be bound to exhibit a strong devaluation bias since deficit countries would be forced by the depletion of their reserves to let their rates go down, while reserve accretions would never force the surplus countries to let their rates go up. They could always intervene in the market. This bias has been mentioned by several people this morning.

Surplus Countries

Let me now mention and expand on another major and crucial area of agreement between Sir Maurice and myself. I quote from the last paragraph in his paper, in which he says the United States and the United Kingdom are "the only important countries where the adjustment process has appeared to be seriously deficient." That is to say, the two reserve-centers of the ill-fated gold exchange standard. I have only two additional remarks to make in that respect. The first is that the adjustment process may be thwarted by, to use a phrase of De Gaulle's, "the exorbitant privilege" not only of the reserve centers but also of the surplus countries. The surplus countries indeed are free under the present system to do the following things:

First, they may accumulate enormous excess reserves as a result of what used to be called in the OEEC "bad creditor policies." That is to say, they may follow unnecessarily deflationary internal or restrictive external policies and maintain an overcompetitive exchange rate.

Second, having pursued bad creditor policies and accumulated large reserves, they are rewarded in consequence by their ability to pursue later "bad debtor policies," and run large deficits without ever having to go to the IMF to ask for assistance, at least for a long time.

Third, they can decide unilaterally to impose deflation upon the rest of the world by insisting on gold settlement of their surplus far in excess of current gold accretions. Or, on the contrary, they may decide freely to invest these surpluses in the financing of one country or another, through dollar *or* sterling accumulation for instance.

Fourth, they can later change their minds and suddenly decide to put pressure on Britain by converting their accumulated sterling into dollars or, vice versa, on the United States by converting their dollars into sterling — which is maybe less likely at the moment — or from both currencies into gold metal at the risk of bringing down the whole international monetary system.

I don't say that they have done this in fact. On the contrary, Germany has probably followed better internal policies, on the whole, than its neighbors. It has financed very generously, maybe too generously, its surpluses through dollar and sterling accumulation. It has failed, however, until recently, to help correct these surpluses through price or exchange rate adjustments. Morally, the German authorities may possibly have been right; one sympathizes with them. Practically, they failed to recognize that they could not be right against everybody else, and that the revaluation of the mark was the only practicable policy and far more feasible and less damaging than the alternatives, i.e. persistent German surpluses entailing inflationary pressures for them and deflationary pressures for others; impossible reductions in wage levels abroad; unwanted price and wage increases in Germany; or a spiral of devaluations abroad, including a devaluation of the dollar. The devaluation of the dollar would be very difficult to endorse as long as the dollar remains the kingpin of the international monetary system and would, moreover, entail, under the present system, an appreciation of gold, whether desirable or not for its own sake.

Reserve-Center Countries

My second point is that the persistent failure of adjustment on the part of the reserve-center countries is not a mere accident, but is, in realistic terms, the predictable, nearly unavoidable, consequence of the reserve currency role assumed by them under the gold-exchange standard. Reserve-currency countries get more rope to hang themselves. They may escape for a long time the full pressure of their deficits, but at the cost of building up a precariously held indebtedness exposing them later to sudden discipline through crises.

I would like to quote here very briefly a few figures to conclude this paper. It is striking to think that in the last year before the First World War for instance, the United Kingdom, having been the first full-developed country in the world, had a current account surplus estimated by statisticians at about 10 percent of GNP. Today the two major financial markets of the world, the United States and the

United Kingdom, have a current account surplus not of 10 percent of their combined GNP — that would be about $100 billion — not even 1 percent of their combined GNP, as hoped for by the United Nations — that would be $10 billion — but a combined current account surplus of somewhere around $1 billion.

I think that this drying up of the ability of the two major financial markets of the world to finance capital exports is something which is extremely worrisome. And yet, of course, their export of domestic capital continues. I think it is very unrealistic and difficult to believe that you can adjust your capital account to your current account by closing down the City or by closing down Wall Street, or by closing down the various programs of foreign assistance and intervention to which dollar and sterling diplomacy are condemned by their world-wide responsibilities. I would like to mention, for instance, that in spite of our huge deficits and the British deficits in 1968, we still exported more than $10 billion of U.S. capital and the British themselves had long-term gross capital exports estimated at 1½ billion pounds — about $3½ billion.

Financing Capital Exports

How could this be done? Those exports of capital were not financed by the current account surplus but were financed initially through the short-term private capital funds normally attracted to a major financial market. When those sources dried up, continuing capital exports were financed by central banks accumulating, taking the overflow of, sterling or dollars. And when this began to create great difficulties recently, they were financed by the Euro-currency and Euro-bond markets. This year they were financed in the Euro-currency market at a rate which I don't believe can be sustained. Our banks borrowed from their branches abroad about $3 billion in two years in 1966-1967, about $3 billion a year in 1968, and in the first six months of this year they were borrowing at an annual rate of about $15 billion. Undoubtedly some of that was fed by American capital that was exported there, but still I think those figures are frightening. And therefore we have been led to all kinds of salvage operations. Mr. Schweitzer himself described the present world monetary system and reserve system as being financed only through these forms of negotiated credits. I have suggested that really we should not speak of reforming the gold-exchange standard — it has been dead for some time. In the last five years, the traditional components of the gold exchange standard — that is to say gold and voluntarily accumulated foreign exchange — went down by about $12 billion. There was no increase in world reserves from these two sources. But you had an increase of about $18 billion from what I would call negotiated reserves through the Fund, through the Basle Agreements and so on.

There is a danger still, but I don't want to go outside the subject of adjustment, that the SDR system might preserve some part of this process by allocating automatically a large portion of the SDR's to the United States and the United Kingdom, and in general I would say that the system will have to be changed later on by deciding that the SDR lending potential should really be put to work to sustain *internationally agreed* purposes, rather than the automatic support of national policies, whatever they are at the moment.

The "Fork"

Finally, if I were to make a comment in relation to the crawling peg or wider band proposals, I would say that I would have neither crawl nor wider bands. I would prefer what I call the "fork." That is to say, I would like to apply the same discipline to surplus and to deficit countries. What I have in mind when I speak of the "fork" is this: each country would define a normal reserve level — I don't think this would be as difficult as it sounds — and a country could deplete its reserve level at a certain rate or increase it at a certain rate, but if this were prolonged and excessive, the country would have to discuss with the Fund what remedies would be applicable to the situation. This, of course, is something that already happens as far as the deficit countries are concerned. When they have lost too much of their reserves, they have to discuss internationally the conditions under which external assistance will be made available to them to defend their exchange rate, if this is appropriate. The surplus countries, however, are never forced into that position, and I think they should be. Therefore, beyond a certain rate or level of reserve accumulation, the surplus countries would also be forced into meaningful consultation with others; and if they cannot agree on appropriate remedies — changes in monetary and fiscal policies, for instance — they should be enjoined from further exchange market interventions. They would have to let their rate adjust if they refuse to adjust their internal policies. Compromises, such as the crawling peg, might have their place here.

The Need for De Facto Stabilization

From that point of view, I would also like to drop a purely academic idea which is probably utopian at this time, but someone else mentioned it this morning. I would very much wish that the Germans would not return as soon as possible to a new legal parity. I think it would be a mistake, nationally and internationally. I would far prefer to have a system in which the Bundesbank tries, of course, to have some kind of stabilization *de facto,* but would not legalize this for some time to come. Remember that was always the case in the past before the institution of the Monetary Fund. When a country felt compelled to change its exchange rate, it did not change it overnight. What it did was to suspend the old parity and then test the market. For example, Poincaré stabilized *de facto* in 1926, but stabilized *de jure* only in 1928. I think that if the Fund were to give members in such a situation a waiver from the obligation to declare immediately a new parity, and say that this waiver is conditional upon meaningful consultation continuing until parity is restored, this would be far more beneficial for all concerned, because under the present system it is very difficult to have meaningful consultations. When Mr. Emminger comes to the Monetary Committee in Paris and is asked to discuss what they will do with the mark, Mr. Emminger says: "Gosh! I don't know, and Mr. Kiesinger himself will not know until the cabinet meets." I think you could have much more meaningful consultations under a system of *de facto* stabilization of rates in consultation with the Fund.

A Lesson from Germany

Finally, I hope that any kind of people who still believe in the possibility of, not *legal,* but *effective* national monetary sovereignty will learn their lesson from what happened to the Germans. Germany finally did at the end of September 1969 what everyone had begged them to do in November 1968. They had to do what they refused to do then. If they had done it in November 1968, they would have saved the world and themselves nearly 12 months of distortions and agony, including possibly the break in the long-term stability which it had achieved in the area of wage levels. I hope that this lesson will not be lost on all of us.

The Fund should be empowered to initiate consultations on an exchange rate readjustment recognized as indispensable to correct a "fundamental disequilibrium", damaging to all its members, rather than be forced to wait — as is now the case — until the overvalued (or undervalued) currency country requests such a change.

Flexible Exchange Rates:
A Transition Plan

WILLIAM POOLE

With the instability of present international financial arrangements no longer a matter of occasional crises but, instead, a chronic condition, increasing attention is being paid to the possibility of introducing greater exchange rate flexibility. Many economists have favored freely flexible rates and the arguments are well known. But these arguments refer only to the flexible rate system once it has been achieved, and there has been little published analysis examining the problems of transition to such a system.[1]

It can be argued that the transition problem is trivial: Let the United States simply announce this weekend that it is suspending all purchases and sales of gold and all pegging activities in the foreign exchange market. A good example of such an approach is that of the Canadian transition to flexible rates in 1950.[2] After a very short period of time — measured in weeks rather than years — Canada's foreign exchange market was operating smoothly and the transition was over. Of course, some will argue that the transition would be far less orderly for the United States, but the pat reply is that people are very resourceful in adjusting to changed circumstances, so that the market will be functioning well within a short time.

Any argument over the ease of transition after a precipitous move to flexible exchange rates by the United States appears to be largely academic because sensible *a priori* arguments can be made on both sides, and there is no evidence to appeal to that both sides would accept as relevant.

Furthermore, and this point is far more important, in my opinion political considerations rule out a precipitous move to flexible

[1] An exception is a recent paper by George N. Halm, "Toward Limited Exchange-Rate Flexibility," *Essays in International Finance, No. 73.*

[2] See Paul Wonnacott, *The Canadian Dollar,* 1948-1962 (Toronto: University of Toronto Press, 1965), pp. 75-79.

Mr. Poole is Economist, Division of Research and Statistics, Board of Governors of the Federal Reserve System, Washington, D.C.

exchange rates. A change as important as the abandonment of the international gold standard ought to be subject to the democratic political process. Under such circumstances the economic problems of transition become far from trivial.

The analysis of this paper takes as given the desirability of a system of flexible exchange rates with no direct governmental intervention into the foreign exchange market. This assumption is made in order to concentrate on the transition problem and to avoid repeating the well-known fixed-versus-flexible rate arguments.

In the remainder of this section, the political constraints which ought to be considered in formulating a transition plan are listed. In section II, a detailed transition plan requiring international agreement and cooperation is presented. But, should international agreement on a plan prove impossible, the United States should be prepared to adopt a unilateral transition plan. Such a plan is devised in section III. The cost of demonetizing gold is examined in section IV. Finally, in section V, several concluding observations are made.

In devising a transition plan, three political constraints appear important.

First, as stated above, decisions ought to be made through normal democratic political processes.

Second, the United States cannot ignore the commitments it has made in connection with the gold exchange standard without injuring its international political position. The United States has pledged to maintain the $35 per oz. gold price and has applied considerable political pressure on some countries to hold dollars instead of gold. To honor these commitments, the United States must enter into multilateral negotiations to gain agreement on changes in the status quo and, failing agreement, must compensate countries for losses they suffer as a result of unilateral action.

The third constraint, one involving a mixture of political and economic considerations, is that a transition plan must protect and, if possible, encourage extension of the progress since World War II on liberalizing international trade and capital flows.

Coming from an economist, these political constraints probably represent a naive view of international politics. The specification of the constraints could and should be refined. But the purpose of this paper is to examine the economics of a transition plan, and so the constraints will not be further discussed here.

A Multilateral Transition Plan

If the usual political processes are to be followed, the first problem is to find a way of averting speculative capital flows responding to foreseeable exchange rate changes during the transition to flexible rates. Some would contend that direct control of speculative capital movements would solve the problem, but it is very doubtful that such control is feasible since it is impossible in practice to distinguish between commercial and speculative trade credit and inventories. Attempts to control purely speculative flows would inevitably lead to complete exchange control.

Crawling Limits

The only possible way to maintain the present state of trade liberalization during the transition period is to insure that the rate of return to speculation is low. And the only way to keep the rate of return low is to adopt a "crawling limits" transition procedure. Under current IMF rules, countries keep their exchange rates on the dollar within one percent of par. Under the crawling limits proposal, these limits would widen, but only very gradually. For example, the upper limit might creep up continuously at the rate of .5 percent per year while the lower limit creeps down at the same rate.[3]

With crawling limits, speculation on the dollar exchange rate would produce a risk-free return of, at most, .5 percent per annum. For example, at the present time it is practically certain that the Deutsche mark would for some time stay at its upper limit in terms of the dollar. With this upper limit rising by .5 percent per year, the most to be gained by shifting out of dollars into marks is .5 percent per annum, but there would be some small probability of the mark becoming weak, thereby producing a loss. A United States interest rate .5 percent above what it otherwise would have been is the upper limit to the interest rate change necessary to completely neutralize the effect of the crawling limit on international capital flows. Similarly, if it were assumed that sterling would stay at the lower limit with respect to the dollar, the maximum return from shifting from sterling into dollars would be .5 percent. However, the maximum return from shifting from sterling into marks would be 1 percent per annum.

[3]This simple formula is modified below because the transition period would be too long if the crawl rate were constant at .5 percent.

The fact that the limits between two non-dollar currencies will widen at twice the rate selected for the dollar limit crawl rate must be considered in setting the crawl rate. A dollar limit crawl rate of .5 percent seems quite conservative and should not introduce serious problems of speculation between two non-dollar currencies. However, even a very modest crawl rate will produce a substantial degree of flexibility within a few years. Using the .5 percent crawl rate and continuous compounding, at the end of six years a foreign currency could fluctuate against the dollar in the band .961 P to 1.041 P, where P is the currency's par value in dollars. Of course, the band for two non-dollar currencies against each other would be twice as large.

The question of how long the transition period should be will be deferred to a later point in the analysis. At this point we will turn to the problem of maintaining adequate international reserves during the transition.

International Reserves During Transition

The transition will only gradually shift the burden of adjustment from the fixed rate adjustment mechanism to the flexible rate adjustment mechanism. It will be necessary, therefore, for countries to hold international reserves during the transition period. Gold and dollars must both be utilized as reserves because there is insufficient gold to use alone. The reserve problem centers around the relationship of gold to dollars. Indeed there is a serious dilemma which must be resolved.

If the dollar price of gold fluctuates, Gresham's Law insures that the good money will drive the bad out of foreign exchange reserves.[4] If dollars and gold are both to be voluntarily held in reserves, then the dollar price of gold must remain fixed forever. Fixing the price only during the transition period is not sufficient since expectations of a change in the price after the transition period is over would lead to the elimination of either gold or dollars from foreign reserves. The dilemma is obvious: one aim of a flexible rate system is to do away with commodity money.

[4]This is not the inverse of Gresham's Law as might seem at first glance. Where the choice as to which currency to use rests with the payor, he will pay with the cheap money and hoard the good so that the bad money drives the good money out of circulation. But where the choice rests with the receiver, he will insist on being paid with the good money and so the good money will drive out the bad. When a deficit country sells reserves in order to obtain the foreign currency needed to intervene in the foreign exchange market, the country buying foreign reserves will insist on buying the good reserves. (On the proper statement of Gresham's Law, see Irving Fisher, *The Purchasing Power of Money*, rev. ed., p. 112 ff.)

The dilemma can be resolved by having all countries share jointly in the gains or losses on gold according to a predetermined formula in which an individual country's gain or loss is completely independent of the total amount of its reserves as well as its gold/dollar proportion. To achieve this independence a transition fund is set up, perhaps under the IMF.

The Transition Fund

The transition fund would work as follows: The transition agreement would assign a quota to each country, possibly the same percentage quota as now used by the IMF. At the end of the transition period, each country would be obligated to pay into the fund a gold assessment. The gold assessment of a country is determined by multiplying its quota percentage by the total stock of official monetary gold. A country holding more gold than its proportionate share would be required to pay in all its gold, but it would receive immediate payment in dollars for the excess over assessment. A country with less than its proportionate share would be required to pay in the deficiency in dollars. Given this formula, the dollars paid in by countries with gold deficiencies would, of course, just match the dollars paid out to countries with gold excesses.

Each country would have a percentage share in the transition fund given by its quota. Following the end of the transition period, the fund would sell off the monetary gold in the private gold market, which governments could enter if they liked, according to a predetermined formula.[5] For example, the transition plan might provide that the fund would auction off the gold for dollars in equal amounts over the course of ten years. The fund would distribute the dollars received from gold sales to the various country "shareholders"; and, after the last gold sales, the fund would have no assets and would be terminated.

Given the likelihood that the free market gold price would fall below $35 per oz. under the pressure of gold sales by the transition fund, each country would want as small a share in the transition fund as possible. The determination of these shares would no doubt be the subject of much bargaining at the transition plan conference.

---

[5]Countries now restricting private holding of gold presumably would eliminate the restrictions, thus increasing the private demand for gold.

The Dollar Certificate

The transition fund arrangement destroys the incentive for countries to switch between gold and dollars during the transition period. However, there is a defect in the plan as described so far: countries have no protection against United States inflation which, of course, reduces the real burden of dollars held abroad. This problem, which would surely affect foreign willingness to adopt the transition plan, can be avoided by creating dollar certificates with a purchasing power clause.[6] All dollar reserves held by foreign governments and central banks at the beginning of the transition period would be converted into the dollar certificates.[7] Like gold, the certificates would bear no interest,[8] and the number outstanding (including those held by the United States) would be held constant throughout the transition period. The United States would stand ready at any time to redeem the certificates for current dollars at a redemption price given by application of the purchasing power clause. The United States could also reissue certificates previously redeemed, but it could not create new certificates on its own initiative. Because of the Gresham's Law problem discussed earlier, the price of official gold must be fixed at 35 certificate dollars per oz., which means that the current dollar price of official gold would be the same as the current dollar value of the certificates.

The restriction of the number of dollar certificates to the initial stock of official dollars is necessary to assure that the certificates remain perfect substitutes for gold. Certificates would become an inferior form of reserves if the United States could issue indefinite amounts to finance balance of payments deficits. United States deficits, if any, would have to be financed by drawing down its gold stock, reissuing any previously redeemed certificates, and/or borrowing abroad on whatever terms could be arranged.

During the transition period, the two-tier gold market should be retained. Otherwise, it is likely that there would be costly sales of

[6] The purchasing power clause could use a United States price index, or a dollar price index of internationally traded goods.

[7] In order to avoid problems during the period when the transition plan is being debated, the plan might provide that the dollar reserves as of the date when the plan is announced, rather than as of the beginning of the transition period, will be converted into dollar certificates.

[8] The United States might pay a small rate of interest on dollar certificates to compensate certificate holders for the risk that the U.S. might abandon its commitments.

private gold hoards to central banks in anticipation of a fall in the gold price when open market sales of monetary gold begin. In addition, since gold production is currently three to four times actual gold usage in industry and the arts[9], it would be costly and inefficient to support the gold mining industry during the transition period.

The stock of world reserves would be fixed in constant dollar terms, while changing in current dollar terms according to the current value of the price index. Given the increasing exchange flexibility, the constancy of world reserves during the transition period should not be a source of difficulty.

The dollar certificate proposal is designed to maintain the real value of dollars held abroad, thereby satisfying one of the political constraints stated in section I. While it is difficult to deny that the dollar certificate is likely to have a more stable real value than a dollar with a gold guarantee, the gold mystique is still strong enough that some may desire that the United States maintain the gold value of dollar liabilities. But it is impossible to design a scheme to maintain both the dollar's gold value and its real value at the same time. The position taken here is that the real value is fundamental.

The dollar certificates outstanding at the completion of the transition period may remain outstanding indefinitely if countries want to continue holding them. The United States, however, should stand ready to redeem them in current dollars at the rate implied by the current level of the price index. Certificates redeemed after the end of the transition period would be retired, never to be reissued. The redemption process would probably be gradual because a rapid redemption and sale of the dollars on the foreign exchange market would depress the dollar exchange rate and encourage some countries to retain the certificates until the dollar was stronger on the foreign exchanges.

The length of the transition period is yet to be discussed. In principle, there is an optimal length for the transition period determined by several competing factors. On the one hand, a relatively high crawl rate would rapidly increase the range of possible exchange fluctuations, thereby quickly shifting the adjustment process from the fixed rate mechanism to the fluctuating rate mecha-

[9]In a recent paper, Fritz Machlup has estimated 1967 production (including U.S.S.R.) at about $2,000 millions at $35 per oz. while he estimates industrial and artistic exhaustive demand (i.e. excluding increases in inventories) at about $500 millions. See Fritz Machlup, "The Price of Gold," *The Banker*, Vol. 118, September 1968, pp. 782-791.

nism and reducing the possibility of a collapse in the international financial system. Furthermore, it is likely to be easier to maintain the required amount of political cooperation over a shorter transition period. On the other hand, a rapid crawl rate would lead to a rapid realignment of some exchange rates in the early years of the transition period requiring countries with initially overvalued currencies to maintain interest rates high enough to reduce capital outflows to manageable proportions; such interest rates might prove more restrictive domestically than is desirable. Finally, the band must be wide enough at the end of the transition period that with high probability exchange rates will be well within the band making it possible to discard the limits altogether and terminate the transition period on schedule.

A few simple calculations may provide some feel for the problem. It seems not unreasonable to require that the limits be at least 15 percent on either side of par at the end of the transition period. Furthermore, it would seem that a dollar crawl rate of .5 percent per annum, which would lead to a 1.0 percent crawl rate for each limit for non-dollar currencies against each other, would be quite manageable in terms of effects on the domestic stabilization policies of major countries. With a .5 percent crawl rate, the limits on the dollar exchange rate would in thirty-two years be 19 percent above and 16 percent below par. But this seems rather too long a transition period.

A more attractive procedure would be to begin with a low crawl rate to allow realignment of exchange rates to eliminate the major disequilibria that exist today, and then to increase the crawl rate in the later stages of the transition period. One possibility would be to set the crawl rate at .5 percent for the first five years, .75 percent for the next five years, and 1.0 percent for the next ten years. By the time the crawl rate is increased, there will have been some realignment of exchange rates and a corresponding reduction in balance of payments disequilibria so that the adjustment to the higher crawl rates should not be difficult. With this schedule, it would take twenty years to achieve the same limits as achieved above in 32 years with a constant crawl rate.[10] With reasonably responsible internal policies, exchange rates should be well within these limits at the end of a twenty-year transition period, so there should be no difficulty in abolishing the limits altogether at that time.

---

[10] After five years, the limits would be 3.4% below and 3.6% above par. After ten years, the limits would be 7% below and 7.5% above par.

Unilateral Action by United States

If an international agreement cannot be reached, the United States ought to take unilateral action rather than support the fixed exchange rate system through a combination of domestic deflation and trade and capital restriction. A plan for unilateral action would also strengthen the United States' bargaining position which would be quite weak if unilateral action were ruled out. Furthermore, the very presentation of a multilateral plan would suggest that the United States has such a pessimistic view of the fixed rate system that it might well act unilaterally anyway. Unless a convincing plan of unilateral action were made public simultaneously with the multilateral plan, fears as to the nature of possible United States unilateral action could cause an immediate exchange crisis of mammoth proportions.

In devising a unilateral plan, the crux of the matter is, as with the multilateral plan, to provide for a gradual transition so that large speculative profits cannot be assured. The basic plan might be as follows: The United States would start lowering its buying price of gold by one percent per year, and raising its selling price by one percent per year. The United States would assume no further responsibility for fixing exchange rates. However, any foreign country that wanted to do so could buy gold from or sell gold to the United States at any time at whatever the current United States buying or selling prices are.

Thus, a country could intervene in the foreign exchange market, if it chose to do so, to prevent a depreciating dollar from causing losses for its citizens holding dollars. The country would be protected with respect to its official holdings of dollars insofar as it was willing to use the dollars to buy gold. If it did not want to buy gold, then its holdings of dollars could be used either to buy United States goods, or sold for other currencies, or simply held. The country could also, if it so chose, sell its gold to the United States for dollars. In this way, the United States would satisfy its many pledges to maintain the price of gold, not by actually maintaining the price, but by giving countries an option of buying or selling gold before the price changed significantly.

To protect itself against the possibility that its buying price would be a support price for the private market, the United States should make clear at the outset that there are limits to the amount of gold it will buy. After netting out United States gold sales to a country, the maximum amount (in ounces) of gold the United States should buy from that country should be the country's official monetary gold stock on the day when the unilateral plan is announced. Conversely, countries might desire to buy more gold than the United States had available. The United States must, therefore, retain the right to redeem dollars in the foreign currency of the country involved. The foreign currency would be obtained either by borrowing from the foreign government or by floating bonds in the country's private capital market. Any country refusing to permit the United States to borrow would be denied the privilege of exchanging its dollars at the price guaranteed by the United States.

If the United States chooses to redeem dollars in foreign currency, the rate should be determined as follows: let $P_{U.S.}$ be the current United States selling price of gold; and let P_f be the par value price of gold in the foreign currency,[11] where the par value is taken as of the date the United States adopts its unilateral plan; and let R be the number of units of foreign currency per dollar; then

$$R = \frac{P_f}{P_{U.S.}}$$

This formula is the equivalent of the United States taking borrowed foreign currency to the foreign central bank and buying gold from it at the price P_f, which remains constant over time, and then selling this gold back to the foreign central bank for dollars at the price $P_{U.S.}$, which rises by one percent per year.

This plan, then, throws to foreign countries the choice as to whether to limit exchange rate fluctuations. But, the United States shares the burden of exchange intervention. The precise exchange intervention points chosen by any particular country will depend on its attitudes toward gold and dollars, and on its forecasts as to future exchange rate and free market gold price fluctuations. Each country will fall into one of three classes.

1) A gold bloc may emerge in which each country belonging to the bloc buys and sells gold at a fixed gold parity. A gold bloc country would prevent the dollar from depreciating below the point at which it can buy dollars and then use the dollars to buy gold from the United States at a net cost in its own currency equal to its gold parity. The limit to the appreciation of the dollar would be

[11] By par value price of gold is meant the foreign currency price of gold implied by a country's declared par value on the dollar, given a gold price of $35 per oz.

determined in a similar manner. If net sales of gold to the United States ever approached the country's limit determined by its initial gold stock, the country would be forced to permit the dollar to appreciate further, unless it could borrow dollars in the United States or elsewhere. On the other hand, if the dollar depreciated and the United States, after running out of gold, began to redeem dollars in borrowed foreign currency, each gold bloc country would have to decide whether to accumulate claims on the United States, the claims being denominated in the country's own currency. It is likely that a country would intervene, at least when the dollar depreciated somewhat below the gold parity intervention point, because the greater the depreciation of the dollar, the higher the rate of return from intervening, thereby inducing the United States to borrow. [12] The intervention points will, of course, change over time as the United States buying and selling prices for gold gradually spread apart.

2) A dollar bloc may emerge in which countries peg their currencies more or less rigidly to the dollar. Such countries would have to hold dollar reserves and to adapt their policies to those of the United States.

3) Finally, a pragmatic profit-maximizing bloc may emerge. These countries would be wedded to neither gold nor dollars, but would hold whichever assets promised the highest return. Since the downward crawl of one percent per annum in the United States gold buying price would produce a negative yield to gold holding while dollar assets would have a positive interest yield, a pragmatic bloc country would probably convert all of its gold into dollars at an early date. Only if the expected rate of increase of the free market gold price were above the United States interest rate minus one percent, would a pragmatic bloc country want to hold onto its gold. As time went on, it would be even less profitable for a country to convert dollars into gold because of the immediate loss produced by the spread between the United States buying and selling prices for gold. There is no natural intervention point to prevent appreciation of the dollar; a pragmatic country would simply sell off gold and/or dollars as it thought best to limit the appreciation. A lower limit to depreciation of the dollar, however, is determined by the point at which it becomes profitable for a country to buy dollar exchange,

---

[12] The rate of return is greater than the nominal interest rate on the loan by virtue of buying dollars at a discount from the gold parity intervention point.

use the dollars to buy gold from the United States, and then sell the gold on the free market. This intervention point may be either above or below the gold bloc intervention point defined above, depending on whether the free market price of gold is above or below the country's original par value price of gold. If the United States is redeeming dollars in borrowed foreign currency, then the intervention point is subject to the same considerations as discussed above for the gold bloc countries under these circumstances.

In all three cases, countries may intervene before exchange rates have moved to what we have called intervention points. Such intervention might take place in an attempt to create more stable market conditions and/or on the basis of purely speculative considerations resulting from expectations as to exchange rate movements.

As the United States buying and selling prices for gold become farther and farther apart, the number of gold transactions will diminish, and eventually there will be no further transactions at the official buying and selling prices. When it is clear that no further transactions are likely, the commitment to buy and sell should be rescinded and the remaining monetary gold stock disposed of by periodic sales on the free market.

Surprisingly enough, the unilateral plan would not seem to violate the Articles of Agreement of the International Monetary Fund if the Articles are strictly construed and so long as the United States does not have to avail itself of the option of redeeming dollars in borrowed foreign currency rather than in gold. The relevant language appears in Article IV:

Section 2. *Gold purchases based on par values*

The fund shall prescribe a margin above and below par value for transactions in gold by members, and no member shall buy gold at a price above par value plus the prescribed margin, or sell gold at a price below par value minus the prescribed margin.

Section 3. *Foreign exchange dealings based on parity*

The maximum and minimum rates for exchange transactions between the currencies of members taking place within their territories shall not differ from parity

(i) in the case of spot exchange transactions by more than one percent;

Section 4. *Obligations regarding exchange stability*

(a) Each member undertakes to collaborate with the Fund to

provide exchange stability, to maintain orderly arrangements with other members, and to avoid competitive exchange alterations.

(b) Each member undertakes, through appropriate measures consistent with this Agreement, to permit within its territories exchange transactions between its currency and the currencies of other members only within the limits prescribed under Section 3 of this article. A member whose monetary authorities, for the settlement of international transactions, in fact freely buy and sell gold within the limits prescribed by the Fund under Section 2 of this article shall be deemed to be fulfilling this undertaking.

Section 2 permits the United States to set a buying price for gold below par, and a selling price above par. The obligation to keep currency transactions within one percent of par as stated in Section 3(i) is, according to Section 4(b), fulfilled if a country freely buys and sells gold within the restrictions imposed by Section 2.

The unilateral plan would clearly not be within the spirit of the Fund Agreement. One of the purposes of the Fund is "to promote exchange stability . . ." [Article I (iii)]. However, the strict constructionist could argue that "exchange stability" is not the same as "exchange rigidity" and that fluctuating exchanges may promote exchange stability and other purposes of the Fund such as,

to facilitate the expansion and balanced growth of international trade, and to contribute thereby to the promotion and maintenance of high levels of employment and real income, and to the development of the productive resources of all members as primary objectives of economic policy. [Article I (ii)]

While the United States would apparently not violate the Articles by adopting the unilateral plan, it might force other IMF members to do so. If other members supported their currencies within one percent of par, they would either have to risk accumulating additional large amounts of dollars, or risk having to take losses on gold as the United States gold price spread grew ever larger. Other members could avoid this problem only by switching to a policy of buying and selling gold freely to members in order to avoid the obligation to peg exchange rates within one percent of par.

The Cost of Demonetizing Gold

Under any reasonable economic definition of cost, for the world as a whole, the direct cost of demonetizing gold is negative; that is to say, there is a positive gain to be had from demonetizing gold. By direct cost is meant the cost of selling off the monetary gold stock to private individuals. The indirect costs and benefits, which result from the monetary stability (or lack thereof) of a gold standard, are the very benefits from adopting a flexible rate system which have been taken for granted in this paper. But since the direct cost is always an issue in any discussion of demonetization of gold, it is useful to examine the issue with some care.

Once incurred, the costs of gold production are irrelevant for future decisions; opportunity costs, not sunk costs must be examined. Ignoring all of the indirect effects concerning monetary stability, it is obvious that, at this point in time, to simply store the existing stock of gold is the most costly alternative. Rather than pay storage costs, it would be cheaper to dump all the gold into the depths of the ocean. Of course, a better alternative exists. The monetary gold should be sold to the private sector at the highest price possible. Whatever the gold brings when it is sold to the private sector will be a net gain as compared to simply letting the gold sit idle in vaults. Assuming that gold lost its monetary demand, both public and private, the price of gold would sink to a level that would create an excess of current industrial and artistic demand over current production, thus using up some of the current stock. This situation would continue over a period of years until the stock was exhausted. The benefits from using up the stock would consist of the release of resources presently used in gold mining and in the industrial and artistic services yielded by the gold as it was used.

While it is perfectly clear that, for the world as a whole, the direct opportunity cost of demonetizing gold is negative, there are still questions of the distribution of gains and losses. Under the multilateral plan, governments would share in the true gain according to the predetermined quotas, while recording bookkeeping losses, since gold would be carried on the books at 35 certificate dollars per oz. and sold for something less. Under the unilateral plan, the United States might be forced to bear some losses on gold purchased from other nations. With a buying price starting at $35 per oz. and declining at one percent per year, the United States could end up buying all foreign official gold at prices close to $35 per oz., amounting to an outlay of approximately $29 billion. However, the United States would realize something on its pre-plan gold stock (currently about $11 billion at $35 per oz.) which would otherwise sit idle in vaults.

Under the extreme assumption that the United States purchased all the foreign official gold, the break-even disposal prices would be $25 per oz.; and, even if the disposal price were $15 per oz., the net loss would amount to only twelve billion dollars. Actually, the possibility that the United States would experience inflation might make countries reluctant to exchange gold for dollars, and some profits might be made through the spread between buying and selling prices for gold. At any rate, the net costs are likely to be relatively small, especially when compared to the cost imposed by monetary instability under fixed rates.

While detailed knowledge of the gold industry would be required to produce any numerical estimates of the effects on the price of gold of demonetization, the formal nature of the problem is clear. First, an estimate of the stock of monetary gold to be sold to the private sector is needed. In the case of the multilateral transition plan, this stock would equal the present official gold stock, since the two-tier gold market would keep the official gold stock at its present size, less any monetary gold purchased by governments from the transition fund. In the case of the unilateral plan, the figure required is an estimate of the amount of gold the United States would have by the time the spread between the buying and selling prices becomes so large that no further transactions occurred. The maximum amount would be the present official gold stock.

For convenience, it may be assumed that the annual sales would be large enough that sales plus production would exceed usage, the difference accumulating in private speculative stocks. This assumption implies that the gold price would be unaffected by the exact size of the annual sales, assuming constant marginal costs of storing gold; so that, for analytical purposes, we may assume that all the gold is sold at once at $t = 0$. Under these conditions, the size of the annual sales determines only who stores the stock, government or private parties, and not the price. It is then necessary to specify the time at which sales would begin.

If private parties are to hold speculative stocks of gold, the gold price must be expected to rise steadily over time at a rate equal to the interest, storage, and risk costs of storing gold. This means that, at $t = 0$, the gold price must be at a level, say P_O, such that there is an excess flow demand (from industry and the arts). The gold price will gradually rise over time according to $P_t = P_o e^{rt}$, where r is the annual rate of carrying costs. Eventually P_t becomes high enough that current gold production just covers the flow demand, thus reducing excess demand to zero, and ending the sales out of gold stocks. At this point, the gold stocks should be exhausted. If they are not exhausted, then the initial P_0 was set too high.[13]

At the current time, production (including U.S.S.R.) is about 57 million ounces per year while usage is about 14 million ounces per year. The accumulated stock, including both official stocks and estimated private stocks, is about 1,800 million ounces.[14] From these statistics, it is clear that, in the event that gold were demonetized and official stocks sold, the price would have to drop far below $35 per oz. The price would probably drop far enough to entirely eliminate gold production for a number of years while industrial and artistic demand worked down the stock.

Concluding Observations

This paper has presented two transition plans, a multilateral plan and a unilateral plan. In practice, it is likely that some, though not all, countries would be willing to join the United States in implementing a multilateral plan. In this case, the plans could be adapted so that a group of countries would adopt the arrangements of the multilateral plan among themselves while adopting the unilateral plan arrangements *vis a vis* other countries.

It is hoped that the plans presented will encourage more thinking on transition problems. Additional analysis is needed to develop the feasible plans of this paper into optimal plans. In particular, the size

[13] The mathematical statement of the problem is as follows: Let the excess flow demand function for gold at time, t, be $D_{Et} = D_E(P_t, t)$; let the stock of gold to be sold off be S_0; and let the carrying costs for storing gold be r per annum. Furthermore, let T be the time when the price has risen to a level such that the excess demand is zero. Since the price trajectory must be $P_t = P_0 e^{rt}$, T is found as a function of P_0 such that $0 = D_E(P_0 e^{rT}, T)$. Let this function be $T = T(P_0)$. We can now write the solution as the value of P_0 such that

$$S_0 = \int_0^{T(P_0)} D_E(P_0 e^{rt}, t)\, dt.$$

Depending on the nature of the excess demand function, multiple solutions to the above equation are possible. In the event of multiple solutions, the one involving the highest value of P_0 would, of course, be the market solution.

[14] These figures refer to 1967, and are derived by dividing the dollar figures in Machlup, op. cit., by $35.

of the limit crawl rate needs further examination. But any transition plan must meet certain basic political requisites. It must be possible to discuss the plan and negotiate its details without causing an international financial crisis. Since the United States would be breaking an implied contract to maintain the price of gold at $35 per oz., it must attempt to negotiate a multilateral plan acceptable to other nations or, failing agreement, must compensate foreign governments for losses caused by a unilateral abandonment of the gold standard.

There is much to be said for the point of view that economists should design programs with desirable economic properties without worrying about political feasibility. But the political requisites discussed in this paper are not mere matters of party or international politics; they involve the basic notions of the democratic process and of compensation for losses forced upon others when previous commitments are broken. Advocates of flexible exchange rates have, so far, almost entirely ignored these issues in their concentration on the steady state advantages of exchange flexibility. But, as this paper has attempted to show, a transition to flexible rates within certain basic political constraints raises important economic problems. These problems ought to be analyzed by economists and not merely left to the political representatives of governments negotiating at some international conference.

DISCUSSION

ELI SHAPIRO

In addition to serving as a discussant, I thought it might be useful if I also attempted to contribute a minor sermon. In the first role I would start by asserting that philosophers, like vegetables, are profoundly affected by their environment. To support this first assertion I would submit the following: in June, 1969 the Federal Reserve Bank of Boston saw fit to call a conference, the major unstated purpose of which can be interpreted to be to mount yet another assault on the "monetarists." More subtly, the June conference could have been called an assault or a call to arms to stop Milton Friedman who had been so effective in boring from within — to borrow a Marxist phrase never used against Friedman before. His (Friedman's) boring-from-within was so effective that it even ensnared such a great 19th century libertarian as Senator Proxmire who was led to demand figures on, and explanations from, the Fed on the money supply for which it was presumably responsible.

We are gathered here this week as guests of the Boston Fed to discuss the international payments system. While I have not yet received and therefore have not yet read all of the papers on the program, I note that one paper is devoted to a spirited defense of the fixed exchange rate system; three papers take for granted some degree of flexibility in exchange rates and are concerned with how to get there or why we should. Of the remaining sessions, I am assuming at least one-half will have something favorable to say about flexible rates and variants thereof. I would guess, therefore, that over 50 percent of the program is devoted to the virtues of yet another thorn in the sides of the central banking authorities — flexible exchange rates!

As a preacher, I could remark about the power of positive prayer. Being Eli Shapiro and not Norman Vincent Peale, my theology was learned in a different department of the university. Hence, I conclude my sermon by remarking flatteringly on the powers of positive economics. While Milton Friedman has had somewhat more allies in his attacks on fixed exchange rates than he did on his attacks on credit markets or whatever variant of monetary policy the non-believers supported, the growth of interest in the subject matter

Mr. Shapiro is Professor of Finance, Graduate School of Business Administration, Harvard University, Cambridge, Massachusetts.

of both Boston Federal Reserve Bank seminars is the greatest testimonial to the courage, scholarship and singlemindedness of Milton Friedman, a man who has often been described as a person with a whim of iron.

In concluding this sermon, I would like to forestall the possibility of the charge of being a sychophant of the so-called Chicago School by freely admitting that in the over 30 years I have known Milton he has gotten as large a share of my blood in debate as he has of others. I do think, however, in a world of attack on the university, the singular success of Friedman is my measure of the need for free and unfettered scholarly research on subjects of great interest to scholars. For indeed, it is hard to believe that 1 percent of the monetary economists in the world, both domestic and international, in as short a period as 20 years would have believed that a June and October conference on their respective themes would ever have been called by a regional representative of the Federal Reserve System. Much as I would like to attribute a major role to Milton Friedman's scholarship, it impinges on me as a scholar to have him share this credit with developments in the environment which have arisen to plague central bankers. Since Frank Morris has already informed us of the subject matter of the proposed third conference, my plea is that for its fourth conference the Federal Reserve Bank of Boston should choose the theme "Was the Plaguing of the Central Bankers Self-Induced or Imposed?" I am convinced this would make an interesting and lively seminar with a prospectively high payoff for the public.

As I see the problems, developments that have been taking place in the environment over the last 20 years have changed and thrown up a set of problems to which measures for their solution are required. Furthermore, as a consequence of both of these seminars, there is a search for more automaticity in the corrections, or corrective responses, and a desire for less dependence on judgment, feel and other intuitive nouns as guides to policy. I believe we owe a debt of gratitude to Bill Poole for wisely choosing to deal with a problem that is often shoved under the rug. As he so correctly points out at the end of his paper, there is a good deal of debate and confusion in the debate which is due to the absence of a distinction between, as he describes it, the steady state flexible exchange rate system and the kinds of problems that might be associated with their introduction. And I think he is quite correct and quite wise in devoting his energies and his intelligence to trying to deal with the transition problem. If indeed he takes for granted the desirability of a free exchange rate, one has to demonstrate the way in which you achieve this state.

Lessons from the Elimination of the Peg

While he has not talked about this, I do believe it is appropriate, before I comment on some of his suggestions, to remind you that one of the issues in the debate is the degree of speculation and upset in financial markets that would result from a change in our fixed rate system. I have often thought that there is a good deal of information to be gained from an understanding of a similar range of problems which surrounded the widespread debate about the elimination of the peg — finally consummated in March of 1951. The standard variant of the debate after 1945 was to see who could make headlines in the *New York Times;* economists are not fools, nor are they loath to accept publicity. So the game became one of announcing that if you eliminated the bond-support program, Government bonds would fall to 80. That got headlines in the *Times,* so the next headline seeker went to 65 percent of par and got even bigger headlines, and ultimately you got down to predictions that bonds would fall to about 46 as a consequence of eliminating the bond-support program. Be that as it may, we eliminated that bond-support program in March of 1951. There was a certain amount of disturbance in the market and the Fed did indeed actively intervene to "correct disorderly markets"; there were a few flurries of difficulty associated with the issuance of the Reifler 3¼'s and in May of 1953 when General Motors Acceptance Corporation put out an issue. The private market was battered for a few days which induced the Fed to enter into the market as a purchaser of bonds. So what you had, in effect, was the elimination of the peg and some intervention in the intervening period to prevent disorderly markets from arising. Now this "poor" bond market that was going to fall apart on the basis of the elimination of the support program has shown enormous durability and viability, to say nothing of the depth, breadth and resiliency in volume. For I remind you that in 1968 there were in excess of $22 billion corporate bond issues gross, a number roughly fourfold the amount issued in 1950. It seems to me the market has been very effective and growing in volume. Moreover, it is not without interest that at the time of the bond-support program 70 percent of the smaller volume of issues was directly placed and only about 30 percent was publicly offered, whereas in 1968 those proportions are completely reversed. I am not arguing this as evidence; I think it is an interesting episode to enable us to get a fix on how viable the financial markets are in response to changes in established practices.

I would infer one lesson from the bond-support elimination. It may be necessary to have a central bank or the monetary authority intervene in the foreign exchange market during the transition from a fixed exchange rate regimen in order to avoid disorderly developments — a point that Poole apparently does not wish to adopt in his particular system. I would presumably grant him his wish to eliminate the intervention after the transition partly on the grounds that Robert Triffin worried about this morning, namely, how could you get agreement among the central banks.

Poole's Plan for Transition from Fixed to Flexible Exchange Rates

Mr. Poole concentrates on the problem of transition from fixed to flexible exchange rates. By the "fixed" exchange rates he does not mean "permanently fixed" rates but the present "adjustable peg" system; "flexible" exchange rates are "completely flexible or freely floating" exchange rates, not including any "limited flexible exchange rates" system such as the crawling peg or the wider band.

Mr. Poole's main ideas for the transition can be presented briefly as follows:

1. Assumption: Desirability of a system of flexible exchange rates
2. Transition Process:

a. *Present System*   *Transition*   *Goal*

| Fixed exchange rates | Multilateral transition Unilateral transition | Flexible exchange rates |

b. Recognition of the importance of political constraints in the transition process

If the United States could get the international cooperation, argues Mr. Poole, the multilateral transition plan would be implemented along the following line:

First, a "crawling limits"* procedure would be adopted to prevent any currency speculation.

Second, a transition fund would be set up to prevent a country

*The "crawling limits" might better be called the "expanding limits" or "double-edge crawling limits" since the limits would expand or crawl both ways in upper *and* lower directions.

from accumulating its reserves during the transition in an excessively asymmetrical gold/dollar proportion.

Third, the dollar certificates would be issued with a purchasing power clause in order to compensate for the weakening value of the dollar reserves due to any inflation in the United States.

Mr. Poole's prescription for the unilateral transition plan follows a different and much simpler procedure. If the transition could not be achieved through international cooperation, the United States would start lowering its buying price of gold by 1 percent per year, and raising its selling price by 1 percent per year.

After a period of time, the gap between the buying and selling prices of gold would be sufficiently widened as to isolate the dollars from gold completely and the dollar would find its own parity with other currencies within the flexible exchange rate system.

Mr. Poole's ideas for the transition are supposed to work in such a way as to "meet certain basic political requisites" (page 25). He emphasizes the fact that any transition plan should meet such conditions as to be negotiated "in details without causing an international financial crisis" (page 26).

Weaknesses of the Plan

However, the weakest point in his proposed plan is the very fact that the plan is perhaps politically almost impossible to discuss or negotiate openly and through "normal democratic political processes" (page 3). His multilateral transition plan would require a prolonged discussion and negotiation on an international scale.

Considering the fact that the SDR's have taken nearly half a decade to be put into practice (and the SDR's are only a "minor" evolutionary step within the existing Bretton Woods spirit of a fixed rate system), I am led to conclude that it would be extraordinarily difficult to make, through a normal democratic process on an international scale, such decisions as to abandon the present gold-exchange standard, adopt a freely flexible exchange rate, and to devise an elaborate scheme for the transition process as envisaged in the paper.

Perhaps a more realistic transition to the flexible exchange rates, again accepting his assumption, might be achieved through adoption of an exchange rate system with limited flexibility on a transitory basis as follows:

Present System	*1st Stage Reform*	*2nd Stage Reform*	*Goal (3rd Stage Reform)*
Fixed rates	Wider band (or crawling peg)	Combination of wider band and crawling peg	Flexible rates

There is another concern in Poole's paper which does bother me a little bit. I refer to his argument that the United States must honor its commitments and therefore must guarantee the gold value of these commitments through the various devices that were mentioned in the paper. There are two sorts of issues that arise here. One of them is the question of guilt. Is the failure of the system exclusively the responsibility of the United States? There seem to be many differences of opinion as to where to assess the guilt and seemingly by giving a purchasing power guarantee, the implication is that the United States is the sole guilty party. Moreover, there is another problem which is raised in my mind for example, for those official institutions who have *voluntarily* converted into gold. That is their decision, and they take the losses and gains associated with it. For those who have been *forced* in some sense to hold dollars instead of gold, there is a question of whether on pure equity grounds, they deserve to be compensated. If official institutions had held dollars instead of gold since 1950, and if we assume that the average interest rate earned was 3 percent on balance, they would by this year have accumulated 75 percent more wealth than they would have by holding gold. If the gold price were halved, they would still be ahead. Moreover, the power of a compound interest table being what it is, if they had only held these dollars since 1960 instead of 1950, they would be wealthier by 30 percent as a result of continuous compounding. It seems to me that there is a good case to be made for the United States charging an investment advisory fee to these official institutions for they would have earned nothing by holding gold.

One of the objectives of Bill Poole's proposal, and one of the constraints on it, is to encourage the retention or extension of progress that the IMF system has made in gains in trade and capital. I think there are two sorts of remarks I would like to make on that. These are my judgments; they are widely debated, I would be the first to admit. I think a great deal of credit that the IMF system gets is richly deserved. On the other hand, it is not all black and white. For it seems to me that subsequent to 1960, and if one looks only at the United States rather than the rest of the countries of the world and if one looks only at the capital account of the United States beginning with the Interest Equalization Tax, one can make a reasonable case for the fact that the IMF system has resulted really in a retardation of what are liberal objectives with respect to trade, with respect to capital, with respect to aid, and other forms of tied grants. So that there is some merit to the proposition, at least subsequent to 1960, that the sort of confusion between means and ends that engendered the IMF system at Bretton Woods would be, in fact, enough to drive Aldous Huxley mad, for the ends are now the means in a perversion of the system — at least in reference to much of United States policy, although not all. Moreover, it seems to me that you impose a rather large constraint on reform proposals if you ask of the flexible exchange rate that it be accountable for growth of trade and capital without reference to the fact that you haven't made as much progress on trade and capital since 1960 under the IMF system. Perhaps you are imposing more of a demand on the flexible system than we are prepared to really impose on a fixed exchange rate system.

Timing Problems

Another thing that is troublesome in following up the interesting discussion of alternatives outlined in Bill's paper is that we really have no specification of the extent of disequilibrium at the time that transition is undertaken. Poole starts with a peg that is crawling at ½ of 1 percent per annum and immediately recognizes that the transition would be too long. He does cite, as an offset to reduce speculative capital outflows, the desirability of an interest rate policy that would presumably compensate for the crawl that was introduced. Now it does make a big difference on how long you have to crawl, and by how much you have to crawl over any given interval for it makes a big difference in terms of the internal political problems of the level of interest rates which is required to offset the inducement to speculative capital outflows. My own particular guess is that with even a ½ of 1 percent increase for a couple of years, coming as it does on the top of our interest rate behavior in the last couple of years, the Federal Reserve authorities might have a very severe political problem in maintaining their independence, given the nature of the biases that are expressed by some of the more vocal members of the Congress of the United States, which I understand is the boss of the Federal Reserve System.

A second problem that arises in connection with the timing is that there seems to be only one thing that Friedman and Bill Martin seem to agree on, and that is that the monetary authority only has a short-run effect on interest rates. Hence, if the adjustment and interest rate policy require a longer period of time the presumption is — both Friedman and Bill Martin would say — in effect we do not have that power if the dimensions of the rate rise are that serious. Now Bill Poole suggests that compounding by ½ of 1 percent would provide a substantial degree of flexibility in the system, and, as I say, that issue turns on what your judgments are as to the extent of the disequilibrium at the time of the introduction of the system. This suggests, in effect, my belief that a realignment of currencies may be necessary first. The problem that arises is how do you get this realignment without putting the cat among the pigeons — that is to say, inducing speculative capital outflow at the time that such a realignment is being considered.

Another feature of the first of the plans is that reserves are still needed, although for a relatively short period of time or as long as the transition period is involved. It seems to be in Poole's system of multinational arrangement that the real dollar amount of reserves is fixed, and under the circumstances unless the peg crawls very rapidly, it may be that the system is sort of choked up by inadequate reserves. One of the problems of the system currently, that leads us to be concerned about it and discuss it, is the difficulty of the reserve creation process under the present system. Now let me say further that in connection with the unilateral proposal of Poole, the presumption is that you would have a growing gap between the buying and selling prices of gold, and over time that gap would be sufficiently widened to isolate the dollar from gold completely and presumably then the dollar would find its own parity with other currencies within the flexible exchange rate system. It isn't at all clear to me whether we can, in fact, achieve such a state of affairs. This is not an economic matter, I think; it is a matter of judgment of the negotiations and the conditions necessary for that unilateral transition plan. For example, there may be political constraints such that it would be highly impractical to have the unilateral announcement by the United States of a process to demonetize. gold. If a catastrophic monetary crisis hit the United States, and the only feasible way out were to adopt the flexible exchange rate, it seems to me that it might be more desirable to announce the separation of the dollar from the gold right away rather than by a protracted process of lowering the buying price of gold 1 percent per year, and raising the selling price of gold 1 percent per year. On the other hand, if there were no such crisis, but nevertheless the United States announced unilaterally its intention of changing the dollar value of gold by 1 percent per year successively, the world might lose its confidence in the dollar and try to shift out of the dollar, thereby creating the need for an immensely difficult rescue operation by the monetary authorities. I suspect that it would probably force the United States to float the dollar right away rather than allow several years of the transition period, as envisaged by Mr. Poole.

Now there is another nest of problems which is solved in a more cursory way than I care to see. For example, the issue of what do you do if you run out of gold. According to Bill Poole, the United States must retain the right to redeem dollars in the foreign currency of a country involved, and the foreign currency, says he, would be obtained by either borrowing from the foreign government or by floating bonds in the country's private capital market. Well, a lot of the problem with the present system is that national sovereigns don't view this as the sort of circumstances which they would permit or else we would have far fewer crises, it seems to me, than we currently have. Finally, in his paper Bill Poole says any country refusing to permit the United States to borrow would be denied the privilege of exchanging its dollars at the price guaranteed by the United States. This strikes me as a violation of the first precept he has, which is a guaranteed gold price. These are a group of concerns. I don't mean in any sense to denigrate the paper. I think the problems dealt with are important — particularly important in a policy-implementation sense. I simply think that more ought to be done with them.

The Case for Fixed
Exchange Rates, 1969

CHARLES P. KINDLEBERGER

Students of current Federal Reserve literature may recognize that
I have borrowed the title of this paper, — with one important change
— from an article by Harry G. Johnson in the June issue of the
Chicago review of the Federal Reserve system, published by the
Federal Reserve Bank of St. Louis.[1] I do not propose to argue with
the Johnson paper point by point, although its author is kind enough
to make the case for fixed exchange rates before knocking it down. I
may be permitted, however, to quote three sentences from it, to
agree with one and a portion of another, and to express what I hope
is reasoned dissent from most of two:[2]

(1) . . . . "the case for fixed rates is part of a more general
argument for national economic policies conducive to international economic integration (p. 14)". I agree with this.
(2) "The fundamental argument for flexible exchange rates is that
they would allow countries autonomy with respect to their use of
monetary, fiscal and other policy instruments. . . by automatically
ensuring the preservation of external equilibrium (p. 12)."
(3) "A flexible exchange rate is not a panacea [agreed,cpk]; it
simply provides an extra degree of freedom, by removing the
balance of payments constraint in policy formation (p. 23)."[3]

[1] See Harry G. Johnson, "The Case for Flexible Exchange Rates, 1969," Federal Reserve
Bank of St. Louis, *Review,* Vol. 51, No. 6 (June 1969), pp. 12-24. (Also published by the
Institute of Economic Affairs, along with a paper by John E. Nash, under the title "UK and
Floating Exchanges," *Hobart Papers,* No. 46, London, May 1969). Note that Johnson
borrowed his title from Milton Friedman, whose paper is noted in footnote 4 below.

[2] I choose not to cavil at what I consider as small imperfections in the paper, e.g. the
contradiction between the suggestion on p. 18 that sterling should belong to a fixed-rate
bloc — either the dollar or some continental currency run by the EEC — and the conclusion
on p. 24 that the pound should float; or the disingenuous suggestion, in the light of the
history of moral suasion by Federal Reserve authorities, that if the authorities know
something that the speculators do not know, they can calm speculative fears by making that
knowledge public.

[3] See Egon Sohmen, *Flexible Exchange Rates,* 2nd ed., Chicago, University of Chicago
Press, 1969.

Mr. Kindleberger is Professor of Economics, Massachusetts Institute of Technology,
Cambridge, Massachusetts.

International economic integration is presumably regarded as a benefit, but loss of autonomy under fixed rates is a cost which outweighs it. Or under flexible rates, the benefit of an additional degree of freedom for domestic macro-economic policy is greater than the loss from suboptimal world resource allocation resulting from the separation of national markets for goods and factors. This sets the terms of the debate in which I propose to show that the extra degree of freedom sought by Johnson is illusory. But note that the case is often made, for example by such an advocate as Sohmen, that the fixed-exchange rate system breaks up world markets because national policies cannot be sufficiently harmonized to operate it without controls, whereas flexible exchange rates, plus forward markets, produce world economic integration. There is a hint of this position in the Johnson paper when he expatiates on the propensity of the market mechanism to produce exactly the kind of forward trading to eliminate exchange risk in a world of flexible rates, and this must be dealt with. The question is whether flexible exchange rates are a second-best solution in a world of frail men blown about by political winds to an extent that the first-best solution of a single world money is unattainable, or whether they constitute a first-best solution in their own right.

A Universal Versus Qualified Flexible-Exchange Rate System

Johnson's paper fails to make a distinction between a universal flexible-exchange rate system and the adoption of flexible exchange rates by one or more individual countries in a world where at least one major currency is fixed or passive. Nor was this distinction originally made by Milton Friedman in his famous *Essay in Positive Economics*[4] which Johnson cites in glowing terms, an omission which, as Professor Friedman now magnanimously concedes, has been productive of much confusion.[5] With his present understanding of the point, Friedman has modified his original advocacy of a system of flexible exchange rates in favor of flexibility for any country that wants it, but specifically not for the United States and

---

[4] Milton Friedman, "The Case for Flexible Exchange Rates," in Milton Friedman, *Essays in Positive Economics*, Chicago, University of Chicago Press, 1953, pp. 157-203, abridged in R.E. Caves and H.G. Johnson, eds., *Readings in International Economics*, Homewood, Ill., R.D. Irwin for the American Economic Association, 1968, chap. 25.

[5] See his discussion in F. Machlup, chairman, "Round Table on Exchange Rate Policy," in *American Economic Review, Papers and Proceedings*, Vol. LIX, No. 2 (May 1969), pp. 265 ff.

presumably not for small ones. (Banana republics are also exempted by Johnson on the ground that they do not have the illusion that the price of bananas in local money is a major determinant of the cost of living, as contrasted with the price of imported goods).

Friedman's change of view, overlooked by Johnson, led to the curious result last May in a television debate between Friedman and Samuelson, which I had the honor of chairing, that I agreed with Friedman on flexible exchange rates, Samuelson agreed with Friedman, and Samuelson disagreed with me. The resolution of this inequality, of course, was that, integrated over time, Friedman had two positions, and Samuelson and I each only one.

The extra degree of freedom which a country obtains by adopting a flexible exchange rate does not come full-blown like Athena from the brow of Zeus. It is not created by an economist-alchemist in his study or laboratory. There is no free lunch, and we are still some distance from perpetual motion. Either the country itself abjures from interfering in exchange market; or its trading partners — or some major trading partners — abstain from interference while the country itself intervenes; or exchange rates are agreed internationally. In the last instance, of course, there is no extra degree of freedom for anyone, and wrong rates may persist unaltered because of failure to cooperate in changing them, as in the French-German confrontations of November 1968 and March 1969. Where a country itself forebears from affecting its exchange rate, using rules instead of management, as Professor Friedman would say, or locking the door and throwing the key away, as it appears to me, the gain in autonomy for monetary and fiscal policy is an illusion. Along with one more variable, there is one more target — the exchange rate. Where a large country agrees to let the country with a floating rate set whatever rate it wants, the freedom for one comes from a loss of freedom for the other.

Freely Fluctuating Rates

Let me dwell for a minute on the case of an exchange rate which is freely fluctuating with no official intervention. It is implicit in the case for floating rates that the "external equilibrium," which comes from allowing the supply to equal the demand for foreign exchange in a free market, is equilibrium not only for the balance of payments but also for other macro-economic parameters — prices, wages, employment, interest rates, etc. There is no justification for this view. A foreign exchange rate may clear the market for foreign exchange but exert pressure upward or downward on prices, employment, and so on.

In Canada, the floating exchange rate was abandoned because an overvalued rate exerted great deflationary pressure on the Canadian economy. Adherents of the flexible exchange rate system, Canadian and foreign, dismiss this case contemptuously as the result of the monetary foibles of one central banker whose monetary policy was mistaken. This will not do. The case demonstrates that a fluctuating exchange rate may not give monetary autonomy but provides another parameter to be controlled in managing the domestic economy. Mundell has said somewhere that floating exchange rates require more careful attention to monetary policy, rather than provide autonomy, because if capital continues to move across a floating rate, in response to changes in interest rates — as was true in the Canadian instance — low interest rates will depress the exchange rate, and high ones raise it. There may be possibilities of fine tuning here, but there is surely not autonomy.

But suppose capital moves not in response to domestic interest rate changes but autonomously — because capitalists do not like government policy in the nationalization of electricity (Italy, 1963), or because of student-worker riots (France, May-June 1968). The list is endless and includes most recently a loss of one-third of the Danish reserves in five days in May 1969, or a Belgian loss of $300 million (15 percent of its reserves) in two weeks at the time of French devaluation in August 1969. The balance of payments would be cleared by depreciation, but the new and lower rate would be likely to undervalue the currency and stimulate possibly irreversible rises in wages and prices. It is of some interest that a well-known advocate of a floating rate for the United Kingdom, Samuel Brittan, notes that it is important to float a currency at the right time, "with very careful internal preparation."[6] Where is the gain in autonomy?

[6] See his "U.K. External Economic Policy," a draft paper prepared for the International Economic Association Conference on Mutual Repercussion of North American and Western European Economic Policies, held in Algarve, Portugal, August-September, 1969, p. 7:

"The great fear about a floating pound is that in the transitional period, while the current balance is deteriorating, the rate would be entirely dependent on stabilizing speculation. If the market took a pessimistic view and import prices rose severely at a time when inflationary expectations were very high, there would be, it is feared, a risk of a cumulative cycle inflation and exchange depreciation on almost a Latin American scale. To offset such cost-inflationary forces by financial policy might require very severe unemployment if it were manageable at all."

Where the country retains control over its exchange rate and can intervene to prevent short-run movements which might work at cross purposes with domestic policy, it obtains its extra degree of freedom — if it in fact acquires it — at the expense of some other country. This is the well-known N-1 problem which makes it evident that a system of N flexible exchange rates for N countries is overdetermined. If one (major) country gives up its control of the rate, the extra degree of freedom of the others is produced, not from thin air, but by transfer. Johnson may be urging other countries, and especially Britain, to move to a flexible-exchange-rate system and leave the United States stuck with whatever rate the reciprocal of the N-1 countries produces. If so, he should stop worrying about the "deficit" in the United States balance of payments, on which he has written so fully, since having lost an instrumental variable, the United States must also give up a target. And he should be aware that he is condemning certain import-competing industries to rather more rapid extinction than they otherwise attend, since it is likely that other countries will continue to embrace slightly undervalued exchange rates, export surpluses, and gains in reserves. I gather that the "new" Professor Friedman is willing to accept the logic of this position, and so am I.

If Johnson wants flexible exchange rates with coordinated intervention by various countries, it is hard to see how different this is from the present position where we try, but fail, to get disequilibrium rates changed by mutual agreement. This is a bargaining or game-theoretic problem with a non-zero solution.[7] It is good that the French finally did devalue in August, and unhappy that the Germans did not seize the occasion to revalue the DM upward. The French had had a problem (DeGaulle) which had made it difficult for them to devalue, and the Germans continue to have strong political forces opposed to revaluation. It is difficult to speak on these matters on which we have little experience, but my intuition tells me that fixed rates with discontinuous changes in parities which are out of line (admittedly not yet a workable system) are as easy or easier to operate than continuous cooperation on continuously moving rates.

_____

[7]Note that circumstances are more important than principle in these matters. In 1932 sterling was flexible and the dollar fixed; Britain opposed currency stabilization and the United States favored it. After the abandonment of the old gold price in March 1933, British official opinion saw the need for currency stabilization, and the United States moved into opposition.

Partial and General Equilibrium

Economists frequently confuse partial and general equilibrium. In partial equilibrium everything else is unchanged. Demand and supply clear the market for a commodity without effects on other demands, supplies, national income, prices, wages, etc., or with effects so small that they can be safely ignored. The theoretical argument for flexible exchange rates comes from the application of partial-equilibrium analysis in which *ceteris* are *paribus;* or from an analysis which is converted from partial to general equilibrium by one or more heuristic devices which may be legitimate in teaching but can be applied to the real world only at great risk.

Such a device, for example, in a two-country, two-commodity world is to fix exports in physical terms in each country so that one unit of exports costs one unit of the domestic currency, both before and after changes in the exchange rate. This builds money illusion and exchange illusion into the system. Or the exchange-rate change is made to produce an alteration in the balance of payments by means of assumed appropriate changes in spending in the system, working in the background to change incomes in the direction needed. Or depreciation raises real interest rates which cuts spending.

In all these formulations, it appears that the balance of payments is being maintained by changes in the exchange rate, but other real variables must be manipulated in the background in the right direction and amount to achieve the final result. The extra degree of autonomy is again illusory, resulting from the addition of a variable, the exchange rate, as if it were independent of other parameters in the system, and there were no feedbacks. It must be recognized that the exchange rate in most countries, and especially those where foreign-traded goods, whether exports or imports, enter significantly into the cost of living, is such a pervasive parameter, linked to prices, wages, credit conditions, taxes, etc., that it cannot be treated like the price of potatoes.

In the third quotation above, Johnson goes on to say:

> ...a flexible exchange rate "does not and cannot remove the constraint on policy imposed by a limitation of total available national resources and the consequent necessity of choice among available alternatives; ..."

How true. Disequilibrium in the balance of payments of an ordinary country — I do not speak of the special problem of a financial center

— is the result of one or more of the following: excess spending, excess money creation, too low a rate of interest, too high prices, too high wages, distrust of the currency.

The first-best policy is to correct the cause of the disequilibrium. Exchange depreciation eliminates a deficit in the balance of payments only as it works to produce a change in the real value of one or more of the parameters, i.e. as it works to cut the real value of money, wages, spending, etc. It assumes that actors in the economy are responsive to money values, but unaware of what is taking place in real terms.

In the "banana republics", this is not the case, so that flexible exchange rates lead to a perpetual chase between inflation and depreciation, with most participants in the drama hedged against any cut in real income by one or another protective device which is triggered off when the exchange rate falls. On this account, Johnson recommends fixed exchange rate and a loss of autonomy for these countries. France succeeds in a devaluation, however, only as President DeGaulle (as in 1958) or President Pompidou (as he hopes in 1969 and 1970) succeeds in enforcing a cut in real wages. The British cannot improve their balance of payments unless they do likewise.

Most economists hesitate to put reliance on money illusion but are ready, even eager, to embrace exchange illusion. In the modern world where the citizens of large countries are as intelligent as those of banana republics, this is unwise. The flexible exchange rate does not operate on the real forces in the system. It is sometimes argued that it provides a cover under which changes in real values can be brought about which cannot be handled under fixed rates. This is the moot but unresolvable question as to whether fixed or floating rates instill more discipline in central bankers and trade unions. But where is the autonomy?

The Case Against Flexible Exchange Rates

The main case against flexible exchange rates is that they break up the world market. There is no one money which serves as a medium of exchange, unit of account, store of value, and standard of deferred payment. Imagine trying to conduct interstate trade in the United States if there were 50 different state monies, no one of which was dominant. This is akin to a system of barter, the inefficiency of which is explained time and again by textbooks. Under a system of freely fluctuating exchange rates, the world market for goods and capital would be divided. Resource allocation would be vastly suboptimal. In fact, such a system clearly would not last long.

What would happen in such circumstance is what happens in every case where there is no money: a money evolves. In prisoner-of-war camps, such money evolved from cigarettes. In the United States, there seems little doubt that New York money would take over. Each state would reckon its money in terms of New York units. New York money would become the intervention or vehicle currency in which all states reckoned, calculated cross rates, and undertook transactions. Montana would pay for imports from Texas initially by converting Montana units into New York money which would be exchange for Texas money. After a time, it would probably pay New York units directly to Texas and have them accepted directly. New York units would become the numeraire in which other currencies were quoted. The price of any other state currency would be expressed in terms of the New York unit, but the price of the New York unit would be impossible to express, since it would be the reciprocal of the price of all other units, appropriately weighted, which is the way "money" is priced.

This is the system followed by the world, with sterling serving as the numeraire prior to 1913, and the dollar from 1919 to 1933 and again after 1934. Individual countries could add to their sterling or dollar holdings by developing an export surplus or borrowing. Leaving aside gold production, which is basically irrelevant, world money outside the leading financial center could be increased only as the center had an import surplus or loaned abroad beyond its export surplus. If such borrowing went so far as to tighten interest rates, say in New York, and after the link to gold had been loosened, dollar creation offset it. In this way, dollar creation regulated the money supply of the world through the modality of the United States balance of payments on current account and foreign lending.

Under any system of flexible exchange rates, the drive to establish an international money is virtually inevitable. Even if central banks could be persuaded to give up the practice of intervening in the foreign exchanges — which I doubt — individual traders among those brave enough to continue in business under the uncertainty would hold foreign exchange from time to time to limit risks, and would almost certainly converge on a single currency to hold as a vehicle currency or numeraire. Under present circumstances it would be the dollar. Gradually with time the traders would exert pressure on their governments to maintain the stability of their foreign holdings in terms of domestic currency. The stable exchange rate system, in my judgment, is inherent in the evolutionary processes by which barter moves to become efficient trading through use of a single money.

The process is not unopposed, not unbeset by other pressures. The natural tendency of the human species to want to have its cake and eat it too, frequently leads to loose monetary policies, especially in time of war or crisis. One hundred percent of the populace, including government, demanding shares of national income summing up to 110 percent or more of the total, each backing its demand with market or political power, produces structural inflation.

Professor Friedman believes that there is no such phenomenon as structural inflation, as he blames central bankers for yielding to the demands on them for more credit when wages are pushed up. This is one way to look at it, though not a very fruitful one. Sometimes central bank and treasury officials initiate inflationary spending or increases in money; at other times, which are worth differentiating from the first, they are helpless victims of irresistible political pressures elsewhere in the economy. If they were to try to resist, they would be replaced. The counsel of perfection which advises potential central bankers to refuse to take the job unless they are granted political independence to resist any and all forces pushing for expansion in the economy is intellectually interesting but not helpful.

In the "banana republics," to use Johnson's phrase, fixed exchange rates are desirable but impossible. The consequence is a race between internal inflation and external depreciation in which all but the weakest forces in the society learn to protect themselves, but money is unable to perform its functions as a store of value and standard of deferred payment. Contracts are written in commodities or foreign exchange; riches are stored in goods, luxury apartments, numbered accounts in Zug. Monetary conditions are pathological, and the choice between fixed and flexible exchange rates is not open.

Where there is monetary discipline, the issue is whether to let the local money supply be determined independently, and in line with local needs, habits, predilections, idiosyncracies, at the cost of some shrinkage of the efficiency of the world's capital and goods markets, and the functioning of the international corporation, or to work to try to reshape local money requirements in the light of the larger system. There is a public good/private good problem here. If the

Phillips curves of Britain and German differ sharply, with Britain having such a strong need for full employment that it is willing to tolerate considerable inflation, and Germany so fearful of inflation that it is willing to tolerate substantial unemployment, particularly that of Mediterraneans, resolution is a serious problem.

It may be necessary after time — if these attitudes are unyielding — to adjust exchange rates. Admitted. In a rational world, however, it would seem unfortunate to break up the world market for goods and capital even temporarily — until a new basis of fixed rates could be evolved, because of such attitudes which should be capable of compromise and agreement on a worldwide rate of inflation. Making such an agreed rate stick in the short run creates serious problems. Again admitted. There is no escape from inflation control through exchange depreciation which only worsens it. Where national differences in trade-offs between full employment and inflation are held with paranoid intensity and cannot be compromised, there may be no choice but to break up the world market.

Rejoinders and Rebuttals

Friedman, Johnson, and especially Sohmen, all believe that the disintegration of the world market can be minimized, or, in Sohmen's view, eliminated by encouraging the development of forward markets. I do not want to go into this topic at great length partly because of the difficulty in its lucid exposition, and partly because I have been arguing the case with Professor Sohmen for about 10 years now without making any dent on his position (nor he on mine). Let me give one side of the case, however, which seems to me irrefutable.

The flexible-exchange-rate scholars suggest that a system of floating rates would not be particularly damaging to trade, capital movements, or the activities of international corporations because forward markets would grow up — covering risks for as far ahead as years — to allow all exchange risks to be hedged. With forward markets, uncertainty as to exchange rates would be eliminated. Hence flexible exchange rates would not be seriously adverse to world economic integration.

I find four holes in this argument. First, and a technical one, forward markets add nothing essential to the capacity for hedging which can also be undertaken by borrowing in one market and lending in the other, earning or paying the interest-rate differential. This assumes perfect capital markets, to be sure, but these are

virtually available to large international corporations. The convenience of forward markets for smaller firms, and the reduction in
transactions costs — both of which may be granted — produce no
change in the theoretical capacity to hedge exchange risks without
forward markets.[8]

Second, hedging does not eliminate exchange risk. Under a system
of flexible exchange rates, a trader faces two risks, one on the price
he pays or receives for foreign exchange, the other the possibility
that his competitors may get a more favorable rate. It is possible to
hedge against the first risk, not against the second. Accordingly,
forward markets or hedging through spot transactions by borrow-
ing/lending does not remove all risk.

Third, as Anthony Lanyi states in a judicious treatment of the
costs and benefits of flexible exchange rates, which, however, comes
out in favor of flexibility, hedging is needed not for particular
transactions, but for activities.[9] Business will not undertake investment in exporting, importing, producing abroad, foreign-security
underwriting, etc., secure only in the knowledge that it can hedge
the foreign-exchange risk in individual transactions. It must have
a sense of where comparative advantage lies over a longer period.
Granted, there are risks of foreign-exchange controls under fixed
rates. This is the *tu quoque* argument used by small boys (which
makes it advantageous to attack first). The issue here is only whether
a system of flexible exchange rates inhibits world integration, as
Johnson asserts, or not.

Fourth, and the issue which Sohmen and I have the most
difficulty in seeking to resolve, forward markets or spot markets with
hedging through borrowing/lending cannot guarantee a businessman
the existing exchange rate before he enters the market since his entry
may produce a change in the rate. Johnson, for example, states (*op.
cit.*, p. 20):

> Under a flexible exchange rate system, where the spot rate is also
> free to move, arbitrage between spot and forward markets, as well
> as speculation, would ensure that the expectation of depreciation

[8]I made this argument to Paul Einzig, who countered that my view of the matter is static,
as opposed to his which is dynamic (*A Dynamic Theory of Forward Exchange*, 2nd ed.,
London, Macmillan, 1967, p. xv). Apart from frictions which may reduce the capacity of
forward markets to provide facilities for hedging, I am unable to see what a "dynamic
theory" of forward exchange may mean.

[9]Anthony Lanyi, "The Case for Floating Exchange Rates Reconsidered," Princeton,
Essays in International Finance, No. 72, (February 1969), p. 5.

was reflected in depreciation of the spot as well as the forward rate, and hence tend to keep the cost of cover within reasonable bounds.

This is protecting a trader against a change in the rate by producing that change, the logic of which escapes me. Johnson and many like him have confused the spread between the spot and forward rates, which is equal to the interest differential, with the cost of hedging, which is the difference between the rate at which an individual calculates a deal will be profitable, and the rate he pays for his exchange. If his calculations were made on the basis of a given spot rate, and he is able to cover through the spot market with borrowing/lending, or through the forward market at the interest differential, his cost of cover is equal to the interest differential, plus or minus. But if the exchange rate moves because of his transaction — and those of like-minded people responding to the same phenomena — the interest-differential fails to measure his cost. He is able to hedge only by moving the rate to such an extent that a change occurs in the current account — imports being cut off by depreciation, for example, or exports stimulated, or by a capital movement — in the present instance a speculative capital inflow.

Any unbalanced movement in trade or one-way movement of capital will change the rate, regardless of the existence of battalions of forward-exchange traders and arbitrageurs, and must change it sufficiently to induce an opposite movement in trade or capital. If there are large amounts of capital eager to undertake stabilizing speculation, the rate will not move far. If not, it may have to move far. Arbitrage cannot accommodate a purchase of forward exchange without an effect on the spot rate. The two forward transactions may cancel out but the spot rate must move far enough to induce an opposite flow of funds, or surplus of current payments, to match the spot transactions of the arbitrageurs.

In Sohmen's system, the spot rate stays fairly steady, but changes in the forward rate induced by direct forward transactions or by the forward half of arbitrage transactions can be offset by trader contracts for future imports and exports, stretching forward perhaps for two or more years. But this requires forward markets for goods of equal length; if not, the traders have exchanged a speculative position in foreign exchange for one in commodities.

In short, forward exchange is one of those complex topics which is reassuring to the lazy analyst, at least on my showing. For all its complexity, it changes nothing and can be ignored.

"Best" and "Best Available" Solutions

Let me turn from digging away at the opposition to something more positive, and start with the best and worst of international monetary systems. The first-best, in my judgment, is a world money with a world monetary authority. The authorities should be charged with regulating the world money supply so as to maintain its value stable, or perhaps declining very slightly each year to stimulate employment. This would be an economically integrated world, with a common set of prices and interest rates, adjusted in all cases for the total or partial separation of some markets for some goods, services, and kinds of investment money — including distance from major markets. The distribution of money and credit among regions or countries would respond to trade and capital flows unhindered by governmental obstacles. It is the system worked out in the United States, and sought — but not yet achieved — in the European Economic Community. It is probable that some redistributive mechanism is necessary to relieve those hardships which the market may inflict on certain regions and industries in this system, perhaps automatically through the tax system, with its different distributions of benefits and costs, perhaps in part through subsidies, subventions, foreign aid, and the like to marginal participants in the market process.

This is an economic first-best in my judgment. Most economists will agree that it is politically unattainable. When economists move from the first best to more feasible if less efficient solutions, however, note that they are undertaking implicit political theorizing in rejecting this or that solution as politically unworkable. There is no rigor, no science, no experimentation, some historical observation, and much intuition in these judgments. But economists cannot dodge the necessity for political theorizing since no one else is available to do it.

Almost identical with the first-best solution is the fixed-exchange-rate system with coordinated policies. According to a theorem of Hicks, two or more goods which have a fixed price can be regarded as a single good. By analogy, two monies which are freely convertible into one another at a fixed rate of exchange can be regarded as a single money. Regulation of the money supply so as to keep the monies freely convertible into one another at a fixed price requires coordination of money creation and extinction, along the lines of the distribution of money under the system of a single money used throughout the world. The gold standard was regarded as such a system for coordinating and harmonizing policies in this fashion, with countries gaining gold through trade surpluses or capital inflows expanding their money supply in some appropriate multiple of the gain, while those which lost gold contracted in the same degree. The gold standard, or a system of credit money with fixed rates, assumes that prices, wages, interest rates, etc., throughout the system will be adjusted to one another, and to the world money supply, by economic forces and not to serve political ends.

Most economists insist that this system has been tried and found wanting, since separate countries do not order their monetary, fiscal, price, wage, etc., policies as called for by the system, but rather respond to local pressures, generally resisting deflation, accepting inflation, operating along Phillips curves, etc., at different rates, and in response to different historical experience and with different mental blocks, so as to make the system inoperable. Most of them focus on the different price experience of different countries, and with the aid of an explicit or implicit theory of purchasing-power parity, call for adjustment of exchange rates, usually on a continuous basis.

Economists, moreover, have little difficulty in agreeing on the worst system. Nth best in a system of 1st, 2nd, 3rd . . . . . nth best, is fixed exchange rates maintained by interferences with movements of trade, capital, and persons (such as tourists). This system confuses the container with the thing contained. Some economists have no difficulty in accepting control over capital movements, so long as tourists and goods are free, on the ground that capital movements are not always dictated by efficiency considerations so much as capital flight from situations which people cannot escape, especially normal taxation.

If the best is unattainable and the worst must be avoided, what is second-best and still feasible? In particular, how much economic efficiency should be traded off against alleged political feasibility in a world where hard political data or even firm opinions on the behavior of political figures in relation to monetary phenomena are impossible to obtain?

Take such an issue as centralization. Most of us amateur, implicit, political theorizers agree that decentralization and local participation are good, but that for some problems, such as regulation of the money supply, central control is inescapable. In the world monetary system, national sovereignty makes operation of an international credit standard impossible, or does it? I have recently read a plea for raising the price of gold by a distinguished economist who bases his argument on the explicit political ground that while gold was wasteful compared to credit money (an economic argument), it was useful (politically) in making the money supply of individual countries independent of the actions of other countries. This strikes me as both wrong and misguided: wrong because the deep-seated forces of the world will be searching for a single convenient money as a medium of exchange, unit of account etc., under any monetary system, whether flexible exchange rate or based on national monetary policies relying on national gold reserves; misguided because an economist has little business making sweeping economic pronouncements based on political judgments. The shoemaker should stick to his last. The economist who finds largely political rather than economic reasons for his recommendations has either run out of ideas to support his prejudices or is in the wrong business.

Options and Choices

If we rule out a world currency with a world money supply established internationally, and a fixed-exchange rate system in which each country has responsibility for establishing its money supply in accordance with agreed rules, such as under the gold-standard "game," the choice of a real second-best comes down in the minds of most economists to a national currency standard, or to flexible exchange rates. Of late, freely flexible exchange rates have been abandoned in favor of either a wide band, i.e., rate fluctuation constrained within fairly wide limits; or a crawling, sliding, creeping peg.

Each of these recognizes that speculation may drive the rate way up or way down and impose burdens on domestic policy, and possibly irreversible movements in prices and wages which should be avoided. The sliding peg, much better than the band proposal, recognizes that there are likely to be many occasions when short-run exchange movements should be constrained but not the long run (the band constrains long-run movements but not short). The question for investigation is whether it is second-best to relax the discipline of a fixed-exchange-rate system and give up the attempt to harmonize national macro-economic policies into a converging world position, at some cost in efficient resource allocation, or to undertake the harder political task for higher economic reward.

There is a choice which Despres, Salant and I have long advocated, and to which Professor Friedman has come around. Professor Friedman regards it as a variant of the flexible-exchange-rate system; in my judgment, it belongs in the fixed-rate stable. I refer to the standard referred to by Professor Edmund Phelps in a recent conference as "How to Stop Worrying and Get to Love the Dollar." It requires the United States to stop worrying about its balance of payments (other than the current account, which is currently in a poor position) and to remove its restrictions on capital movements. Other countries can adopt whatever exchange rate they choose. Professor Friedman would recommend that Britain, Germany, and France follow policies of freely floating rates. I would leave it up to them but, as a betting man, be prepared to make a small wager that they would continue, as in the past, to keep their currencies fixed in terms of dollars, even after the withdrawal of such inducements as the German-United States military offset agreement. If I proved to be wrong in the short run, moreover, I would be prepared to bet that in the long run the convenience of maintaining reserves in the dollar, the world's numeraire, a money's money, would be so compelling that they would again stabilize.

To achieve the integration I seek and to limit risks, it would be advisable for countries to indicate to the world whether or not they intend to stabilize their currencies. With those which did so seek, I have recommended elsewhere that the United States seek to work out common monetary policies, so as to defuse the dollar standard from the political dynamite of an imposed dollar standard. The details lie outside the scope of this paper.

In short, I regard as 3rd best, with a chance of its achievement, a dollar standard managed internationally since I judge unattainable the first-best world money and world central bank; and the second-best fixed-exchange-rate system with independently-operated national monies. Fourth best is the crawling peg. The flexible exchange rate system is well down the list.

DISCUSSION

MILTON FRIEDMAN

I should say in advance that I have one great advantage over you people. I had a text of Charlie's paper beforehand and, since he only read part of it, I have a larger collection of fallacies from which to choose than you do.

I may say at the outset that I am amused by two general points. Charlie stressed that the case for fixed exchange rates is the same as the case for a money's money. As he said that, I started listing in my mind the names of people who are for fixed rates and those who are for flexible rates, and also the names of people who have put great emphasis on the importance of money. As I think most of you will agree if you think of those names, there is almost a one-to-one correspondence. The economists who have put most emphasis on the importance of money are flexible exchange rate people. The economists who have favored fixed rates have put least weight on the role of money. So it should give us a little pause whether it can really be so obvious that the case for fixed rates is the case for money.

The second general point is that never in my wildest dreams did I think that I was going to be subject to attack on the grounds that I gave undue weight to political feasibility in making policy recommendations.

One other introductory comment. I want to warn you that there is a real problem of avoiding cases of mistaken identity in reading or listening to Charlie's paper. He refers to somebody by the name of Friedman in the paper — but there are two Friedmans in his paper. I recognize one of them. The other fellow I've never met; I don't know who he is, so I don't know where Charlie got the idea he had the ideas he attributed to him. A second case of mistaken identity is that there are also two Johnsons. There is one Johnson from whom there are quotations, and I recognize the quotations. They are from my colleague Harry Johnson whom I know very well. There are other ideas, that I know my colleague Harry Johnson does not have, that are also attributed to a Johnson. So that must be still another Johnson. To add to the difficulties, there are two Kindlebergers. Statements made in one part of this paper by the author whose name is Kindleberger are inconsistent with statements made in other parts of the paper. So somehow Charlie and his twin brother must have

109

drafted different parts of this paper. Let me start with this final point because it helps to illustrate some of the others.

A System of Universal Flexible Rates versus Some Flexible Rates

At the beginning of his paper — and this is a sentence which he read — he said, "Johnson's paper fails to make a distinction between a universal flexible exchange rate system and the adoption of flexible exchange rates by one or more individual countries in a world where at least one major currency is fixed or passive". Let me spell that out a bit. Let's take the case where one major — not *at least,* but *exactly* one — major currency is fixed. Then Charlie says that there is a distinction between a world of universal flexible rates and a world where every country but one has flexible rates. That is the statement on page two to three of his duplicated text. Later on, on page six, Charlie says — and this is a sentence that he did not read — "This is the well-known N-1 problem which makes it evident that a system of N flexible exchange rates for N countries is over-determined." Now that statement is correct. If there are N countries, there are N-1 independent rates. The first distinction that I read simply doesn't exist. A universal flexible exchange rate system is the same as and not different from a system in which one exchange rate is fixed. If I have two currencies, A and B, I don't have two different exchange rates. It is not possible for both A/B and B/A to go up. If A/B goes up, B/A goes down, and one Kindleberger recognizes that in the second statement that I quoted. It is a good thing that Johnson didn't make the distinction that the other Kindleberger criticizes him for not making because it's not a valid distinction.

The other Kindleberger goes on to say, "Nor was this distinction originally made by Milton Friedman in his famous *Essay in Positive Economics,* an omission which, as Professor Friedman now magnanimously concedes, has been productive of much confusion". Kindleberger attaches a footnote to this sentence referring to a brief paper of mine in the latest *Proceedings* volume of the *American Economic Association.* Let me read to you what I actually said, and see if you can find any relationship between that statement and the statement Charlie attributes to me. What I said was, "The discussion of these issues has been confused on both sides — and I plead guilty to contributing to this confusion — by failure to keep sharply separate the options that are available to a single country and those that are available to the international community". That is a very different distinction than the one Charlie attributes to me. I go on to say, "The critics are right that the U.S. cannot on its own float the dollar in the fullest sense of that term. Hence, I no longer describe my policy recommendation for the U.S. in those terms." Charlie says I have two different positions — before and after. That isn't what these words say. What they say is that I now think that my earlier description of my one policy position was not a good description. It was a description that led to some confusion, because I talked about what was desirable for all countries together, and I did not separate out what a single country could do.

I now believe that it reduces the confusion to separate sharply what one country can do from what all countries can do. But the system that I favor now is identically the same as the system I favored at an earlier date. I went on in my AEA comment to say that what the U.S. alone can do, and what I continue to believe it should do, is to set the dollar free by ceasing to peg the dollar. It can leave it up to other countries whether the dollar floats or whether they link their currencies to the dollar. That is one example of the two different Friedmans that you have to keep separate in Charlie's exposition.

World Integration

As to Professor Johnson — the two different Johnsons — there is one Johnson who is quoted on the first page of Charlie's paper and Charlie read this in his verbal statement: "The case for fixed rates," says Professor Johnson, "is part of a more general argument for national economic policy conducive to international economic integration." Johnson never said that was a valid case. He said those who make the case make it in these terms, and that is true; those are the terms in which they make it. Says the other Kindleberger about Mr. Johnson, and this sentence he did not read: "A system of flexible exchange rates inhibits world integration as Johnson asserts." I challenge Charlie to find a sentence in which Johnson asserts that a system of flexible exchange rates inhibits world integration. There certainly are circumstances under which fixed rates might promote world integration, but there are other circumstances under which fixed rates might reduce world integration. It isn't a simple matter — fixed rates, integration; flexible rates, disintegration. It depends critically on what the other circumstances are. It is perfectly possible for a man to say that those who argue for fixed rates are doing so in the desire to attain world integration. I believe that many fixed rate advocates have world integration as an objective. So do I. I, therefore, approve of their objective. But I say, and Harry Johnson says, they are reaching a wrong conclusion if they believe that the best way to promote that desirable objective today is by a system of fixed rates of the kind that you are likely in fact to have.

But let me turn to more significant matters than cases of mistaken identity. In connection with much of Charlie's argument, I was reminded of the old story about the man who saw a friend of his looking on the ground under a light. He asked him what he was doing. His friend said he was looking for some keys that he had lost. Asked the man, "Did you lose them here?" "No," said his friend, "I lost them up there." "Why are you looking here?" "This is where the light is." Charlie provides all the good arguments for one system which is where the light is: a system of unified world money. That would be a good system, that I would favor. He then implies that the arguments that are valid for a unified world money also hold for a completely different system — a system of national currencies linked by fixed exchange rates. In my opinion, the most important single confusion in the whole discussion of exchange rates is precisely this confusion between a unified currency on the one hand — what we have in the U.S. among the different states — and a collection of national currencies with separate national monetary authorities linked by pegged exchange rates — what we have under what is called the fixed rate system but is in fact an adjustable peg system. Let me turn more specifically to Professor Kindleberger's arguments.

Causes of Disequilibrium in a Country's Balance of Payments

I have already pointed out his confusion between two distinctions: what one country can do versus what all countries can do, and a system of universal flexible rates versus some flexible rates. Let me turn to the logical validity of some of his other statements. Says Professor Kindleberger, "Disequilibrium in the balance of payments of an ordinary country is the result of one or more of the following things: excess spending, excess money creation, too low a rate of interest, too high prices, too high wages, distrust of the currency."

In the first place, most of those terms are undefined and undefinable. What is too high prices? Too high relative to what? Implicitly, Kindleberger has a proper exchange rate in the back of his mind. Too high wages, relative to what? Secondly, and more important, even if we could define each of these terms precisely, a disequilibrium in the balance of payments of an ordinary country need not reflect a single one of these things. Consider a country that is engaging in none of these things; it has no excess spending, it has no excess money creation, it does not have too low a rate of interest, it does not have too high prices, it does not have too high wages, and there is no distrust of currency. But other countries engage in inflationary or deflationary monetary policies. If our hypothetical paragon of a country held the exchange rate fixed, it would clearly have a balance-of-payments problem that doesn't derive from any of the things listed by Kindleberger. So his assertion is a fallacy.

Solutions

Next Kindleberger says, "The first-best policy is to correct the cause of disequilibrium." Nonsense. For our paragon of a country, doing what it can do, the first-best policy is to adjust its exchange rate. It has the right wages and the right prices in terms of its own currency; it has the right relative wages and the right relative prices under the former conditions of demand and supply of foreign exchange. The first-best answer on its part is to adjust the exchange rate to offset the inflationary or deflationary policies of other countries so that it can go on in proper equilibrium without having to engage in completely unnecessary internal adjustment. This particular example is also a counter-example that proves the fallacy of Charlie's next statement. He said, "Exchange depreciation eliminates a deficit in the balance of payments only as it works to produce a change in the real value of one or more of the parameters, i.e., as it works to cut the real value of money wages spent."

In the example I just cited, the paragon of a country that was in initial equilibrium had everything right. It was not necessary for the country to change the real value of money wages or spending or anything else when the other countries inflated or deflated. It simply had to change the exchange rate in order to prevent undesirable changes in the real value of money wages. So Professor Kindleberger's assertion is simply false.

As a final example of a logical fallacy, Kindleberger says, "it assumes" — that is, the proposition that exchange depreciation eliminates a deficit in the balance of payments — "that actors in the economy are responsive to money values but unaware of what is taking place in real terms." That is wrong. For exchange rate changes to produce equilibrium does not require any form of money illusion whatsoever. A system of equations can be expressed in terms of real magnitudes, including the rate of exchange between one country and another, including the real terms of trade, and so on. It does not require any money illusion on anybody's part for such a system to be in equilibrium, as I just illustrated with my particular example of a paragon of a country.

The proposition that exchange depreciation eliminates a deficit in the balance of payments only insofar as there is money illusion is offered by Kindleberger as a logical proposition in economic theory. But you cannot find it in any theoretical treatment of the problem of exchange rates or international trade because it is fallacious.

Let me turn to a different issue, skipping some of Charlie's paper to conserve your time and your patience and give Charlie a chance to beat me back.

Less Exchange Risk under Fixed Exchange Rates?

Let me turn to what I regard as probably the most important single issue involved in the argument for and against flexible rates. It is the issue brought up by Charlie when he asserted that the essential case for fixed exchange rates and against flexible exchange rates is that there is less exchange risk under fixed exchange rates than there is under flexible rates. That is, he said, the essential argument. It's the argument to which he devoted all of his discussion about various forms of forward hedging. It is the argument that Sir Maurice Parsons presented this morning in talking about the problem of capital flows.

In respect of this argument, I feel as if this is one of those continuous movies, and that this is where I came in 20 years ago. In 1950, when I wrote the article that Charlie refers to, "The Case for Flexible Exchange Rates," I took seriously the argument that there might be destabilizing speculation — that is really what Kindleberger's and Sir Maurice's arguments come down to. It is now 20 years later. There has been an enormous amount of empirical work done on this issue. In a debate a couple of years ago with Bob Roosa, I challenged him — and now I challenge Professor Kindleberger and I challenge Sir Maurice Parsons — to provide not assertion, not fears but some empirical evidence that shows that such consequences do flow from flexible rates.* Destabilizing speculation is a theoretical

*See Milton Friedman and Robert V. Roosa, *The Balance of Payments: Free Versus Fixed Exchange Rates,* (Washington, D. C.: American Enterprise Institute, 1967), esp. pp. 105-107.

possibility, but I know of no empirical evidence that it has occurred even as a special case, let alone as a general rule.

How can this be? Isn't it obvious that fixed rates remove risk and flexible rates increase exchange risk? Not at all. The amount of uncertainty that there is to be met is unchanged. The difference between the two systems is the form that the uncertainty takes. Under a fixed rate system, the uncertainty takes the form of whether there will be major exchange rate changes every 5 or 10 years; it takes the form of whether there will be exchange controls; of whether there will be restrictions on imports and exports; of whether you will be able to get your money out. It does me little good to know that if I can get my capital out, it will be at a fixed rate, if I also know that I am likely not to be permitted to get it out just when that fixed rate would be most advantageous. So the fact is that under fixed rates there are exchange uncertainties.

What do these exchange uncertainties arise from? They arise from variations in the real forces affecting international trade that are sometimes favorable, sometimes unfavorable to a country. They arise from the adoption of different monetary policies by different countries; the adoption of different fiscal policies; elections; earthquakes — all these sources of uncertainty are present, whether you have fixed or flexible rates. The difference is that if you have flexible rates, the uncertainty manifests itself in changes in the price of exchange. It manifests itself promptly but gradually, in a way to which people can adjust promptly. When you have fixed rates, the uncertainty manifests itself in exchange and trade controls, in restrictions on what you can do, in large discontinuous changes in exchange rates from time to time.

One manifestation of uncertainty may well be more disturbing to international trade than the other. If you ask yourself which you would expect to be more disturbing, I think all of our experience suggests that the manifestation under fixed rates would be expected to be more disturbing than the manifestation under flexible rates. Why? Because we have observed over and over again that governmental intervention to peg a price, whether it be of wheat, or housing space, or any other good, produces much more serious problems of adjustment than fluctuations in prices. Businessmen all over the world have been able to cope with widely changing prices far more readily than with governmentally fixed prices on railroads, let alone with governmentally fixed exchange rates. So you would expect that uncertainty would be less disturbing to business, to capital movements and to trade movements under flexible than under fixed exchange rates.

If we look at the empirical evidence, and I think I have looked at all the studies that have been published, I do not know of a single documented case in which flexible rates have in fact been accompanied by destabilizing speculation. I sometimes feel like giving the standard reply in poker to a man who is hesitating whether to meet a raise: "Put up or shut up." It seems to me it is about time for those people who argue that uncertainty is less disruptive to trade and capital movements under fixed rates than under flexible rates to give us some evidence or else to stop making the assertion that it is.

Hedging Long-term Capital Movements

One further point on this issue. The persistence of capital movements and trade movements with flexible rates does not, in my opinion, depend very critically on the existence of sensitive and far-flung forward markets. I may not agree with Charlie's long disquisition on forward markets, but I do not regard the problem it raises as very serious. Even if I accepted every word he said, it wouldn't bother me, because that isn't the way long-term capital movements are hedged anyway. The fundamental hedging in long-term capital movements between countries, as within a country, comes from the fact that the investment is made in real terms not nominal terms. If I invest for 20 years from now in a British industry, and if the British exchange rate depreciates to 1/10 of its present value in terms of dollars over the next 20 years, the odds are enormous that the reason will be because British prices in sterling have risen over that period by a corresponding amount relative to U.S. prices in dollars. As a result, the exchange rate will be less favorable but I will have a larger amount of pounds to convert into dollars. That is the fundamental hedge in all long-term capital investment whether between countries or within a country. And you do not need any further forward market for long-term hedging. As a result, I conclude that there is every reason to believe that in the world as it now exists, and as it is likely to exist, a fixed rate system will be more disruptive to capital movements and to trade than a flexible rate system.

The Best International Monetary System

I come to Page 16 of Charlie's paper and to a sentence that he read that I want to comment on. He says that he is going to talk about the best and the worst in the international monetary system. He says, "The first best in my judgment is a world money with a world monetary authority." Now, I will agree with that sentence if he will let me add three letters. I want to make it read, "The first best in my judgment is a world money with*out* a world monetary authority." Now *that* is the fundamental issue.

A unified currency is a currency among political units that do not have separate monetary authorities. Given that you have a world with separate national governments, I cannot believe that anyone who thinks this issue through carefully — on a political as well as economic level — will be in favor of a real world monetary authority. To anybody who has the impression that he is in favor of a real world monetary authority, I recommend very highly *Souvenirs d'un Gouverneur de la Banque de France* by Emile Moreau, edited by Jacques Rueff, and published about 15 years ago (Paris: Génin, 1954), telling about the attempted cooperation from about 1925 to 1928 or 1929 among the great central banks of Britain, of France, of Germany and of the United States. That book, I may say, was the final clincher in persuading me that I was opposed to a world monetary authority.*

A world monetary authority is a politically irresponsible authority which does not have a representative relation to the people of the world. At best, it is a benevolent dictatorship of "experts" chosen in an arbitrary way and subject only very indirectly if at all to any effective political process. A world money with a world authority is, I believe, the worst best and not the first best on both political and economic grounds. On the other hand, a unified world money without a monetary authority would be a pretty good system. I have no objection to that. If people everywhere want to use gold or peanuts or anything else as money, that is not a bad system. That is not a system that can be manipulated or that will have many of the defects I have talked about.

How to Change Exchange Rates

In fact, Charlie recognizes that what he is talking about is not a unified world monetary system, with or without a world monetary authority, but a system in which exchange rate changes occur

*See my article, "Should There be an Independent Monetary Authority?", reprinted in my *Dollars and Deficits* (Englewood Cliffs, N.J.: Prentice-Hall, 1968), pp. 173-194.

discontinuously from time to time. He states the issue on Page 18, in the usual, "When did you last beat your wife?" form. He says, "How much economic efficiency should be traded off against alleged political feasibility in a world where hard political data or even firm opinions on the behavior of political figures in relation to monetary phenomena is impossible to obtain?" I believe that that states the issue incorrectly. The issue is not whether you are for or against economic integration or for or against economic efficiency. The fundamental issue, as I have tried to stress again and again, is how to have exchange rate alterations. Is the most effective way to peg a rate, go through all sorts of contortions and manipulations to try to maintain it, and then finally change it by a large amount in the disruptive fashion we have observed? Or is better to let rates be free to move, to let individuals separately make whatever arrangements and deals they wish with other individuals? I believe that the latter gives you a much greater chance to reduce barriers to trade. In my opinion, one of the major arguments for a flexible exchange rate system — and here I come back to one of the earlier points that Charlie made that I have dealt with implicitly but not explicitly — is that it makes the case for free trade clear and simple. If you have a flexible rate and you reduce tariffs, movements in the exchange rate will automatically protect you against having any adverse balance of payments effects, and therefore you are not exporting or importing unemployment.

Professor Kindleberger says, "The gain in autonomy for monetary and fiscal policy is an illusion. Along with one more variable there is one more target, the exchange rate." This is another of the logical fallacies in this paper. If you have a pegged exchange rate, keeping that exchange rate pegged is a target and you don't have the exchange rate as a variable. But if you say you don't care what the exchange rate is going to be then it does truly become a variable and you are not adding any targets. On the contrary. Under the fixed exchange rate system, you have to use the price level, or employment, or exchange control, or restrictions on imports or exports or fiscal policy — some one or other of your instruments — to achieve the target exchange rate. But if you let the exchange rate go free, you add a variable without a target, provided you are willing to let the exchange rate settle where it will. It is because you have this additional degree of freedom that you do get a greater degree of autonomy in internal policy, and, in particular, you can use it to reduce or eliminate restrictions on international trade.

I want to end by quoting from myself in order to give you the other side of the statement Charlie made at the end, saying that I have come around to a choice that he has long advocated. Well, there is a difference of opinion about who has come where. Let me just quote from some testimony I gave to Congress about seven years ago. "In the meantime we adopt [in order to maintain our fixed exchange rate system] one expedient after another, borrowing here, making swap arrangements there, changing the forms of loans to make the figures look good. Entirely aside from the ineffectiveness of most of these measures, they are politically degrading and demeaning. We are a great and wealthy nation. We should be directing our own course, setting an example to the world, living up to our destiny. Instead we send our officials hat in hand to make the rounds of foreign governments and central banks; we put foreign central banks in a position . . . to exert great influence on our policies; we are driven to negotiating with Honk Kong and with Japan [as you see, seven years haven't changed that one] and for all I know, Monaco, to get them to limit voluntarily their exports. Is this posture suitable for the leader of the free world?" In a more recent Newsweek piece (January 29, 1969), in which I quoted this paragraph, I went on to say, "We should say instead to the people of the world: a dollar is a dollar. You may borrow dollars in the U.S. or abroad from anyone who is willing to lend. You may lend dollars in the U.S. or abroad to anyone who is willing to borrow. You may buy dollars from or sell dollars to anyone you wish at any price that is mutually agreeable. The U.S. Government will not interfere in any way. On the contrary, it will dismantle immediately its present restrictions: repeal the interest-equalization tax; dissolve the cartel agreement among banks to restrict foreign lending; remove quotas 'voluntary' or otherwise on imports; stop resorting to World War I emergency legislation to threaten with prison terms businessmen who invest abroad; refrain from interfering with the right of its citizens to travel when and where they will.

"If a foreign country wishes to peg the price of its currency in terms of dollars, we should not interfere."

That is the point that I emphasize and it involves a valid distinction between what one country can do alone and what a group of countries can do. I would urge other countries that they too would benefit if they would let their exchange rates go free. And if they did that, we would really be on our way to world integration because that is the only route that anybody has so far suggested that will enable us to make a start on dismantling our host of barriers to the movement of men, of goods and of capital.

Widening the Band for Permissible Exchange Rate Fluctuations

GEORGE N. HALM

Our present international monetary system tries to combine three features: (1) fixed par values, (2) full convertibility, and (3) full employment plus stable prices. The member countries differ somewhat in their aims, their policy mixes and their rates of inflation. Moreover, these discrepancies are no longer ironed out over time by the international monetary mechanism itself. No country is willing to embark on inflationary or deflationary policies merely to maintain external balance.

L. Albert Hahn used to speak of the "magic triangle" to indicate that only a magician's wand could make such a system work. Repeated financial crises and growing quantitative restrictions have shown that the system does not work very well though opinions differ as to the reason why. A closer look at the three sides of the triangle can reveal the main weaknesses of the present international payments system.

Stable Prices

Domestic inflation is mainly the outgrowth of monopolistic pressures in the modern market economies which have greatly weakened the downward flexibility of wages and prices. Since the market economy rests on reactions to price changes, and prices are more ready to rise than to fall, the world trend is inflationary though not uniformly so in different countries. Furthermore, it has become increasingly difficult to induce individual countries to adjust their policies to the average rate of world inflation. Surplus countries with full employment are unwilling to increase inflationary pressures in order to balance their international accounts, and deficit countries in recession are most reluctant to use monetary contraction to protect their foreign exchange reserves. These are the dilemma cases in which

Mr. Halm is Professor of Economics, Fletcher School of Law and Diplomacy, Tufts University, Medford, Massachusetts.

policies for the achievement of domestic aims conflict with measures which would lead to external balance. For instance, high rates of interest to stop inflationary pressures in a surplus country attract funds from a deficit country which carries through expansionary monetary and fiscal policies. The balance-of-payments disequilibrium increases in both countries.

If exchange rates remain fixed, currency convertibility is maintained, and domestic policies are not used to achieve external balance, three possibilities are left: (1) liquidity reserves can be increased to permit temporary maintenance of a basically untenable position; (2) refinements of monetary and fiscal policies may accommodate simultaneously both domestic and international aims by carefully doctored policy mixes; and (3) incomes policies can try to achieve what monetary policies were not permitted to accomplish. None of these policies is promising. The first, liquidity creation as stop-gap, may make things worse by permitting postponement of urgent corrections in national economic policies or in par values. The second, the use at cross purposes of, say, contractionist monetary measures for external balance and of expansionist fiscal policy for domestic purposes, may never work owing to the extreme fungibility of money. And, even if such sophistication and fine-tuning were possible in the future, it is certainly not now available. The third, an incomes policy, may be used in emergencies but can never be a long-run substitute for adequate monetary and fiscal measures.

If none of these alternatives will work, either fixed exchange rates or convertibility will have to be sacrificed.

Currency Convertibility

A system of currency convertibility at fixed par values implies that the central banks maintain a perfectly elastic demand for, and supply of, foreign exchange. Liquidity reserves will continuously change. These international liquidity reserves give elasticity to an otherwise rigid payments system. Bretton Woods emphasized this aspect of elasticity by concentrating on the supply of liquidity reserves. Also, most of the more recent attempts to shore up, or to permanently improve, the Bretton-Woods system concerned themselves almost exclusively with liquidity creation. Throughout, not enough attention was paid to the adjustment problem, though it is obvious that the demand for international liquidity depends largely on the functioning or malfunctioning of the adjustment process.

Adjustment can be achieved either through domestic monetary policies which, in dilemma cases, are certain to be inadequate or it can be the result of exchange-rate variations which are excluded by definition as long as we stipulate a system of permanently fixed parities.

If exchange-rate variations are not permitted, if domestic monetary policies are not able to achieve external balance, and if liquidity reserves are inadequate, currency convertibility becomes impossible and quantitative restrictions will be introduced. To maintain fixed exchange rates by quantitative restrictions means to defend the use of a mere instrument by giving up the very aim for which the instrument was designed.

Fixed Exchange Rates

The absurdity of this situation in which controls are introduced to permit the maintenance of a fixed price is well known to the student of government interference with market processes. As a rule, such interferences are only tolerated in national emergencies. In normal times, they are rejected because they prevent the functioning of the market mechanism, the allocation process on which the private enterprise economy depends.

Why then the great reluctance to let flexible exchange rates perform the function of real market prices? The reason is probably to be found in the mistaken attempt to extend the official price stability of domestic money ("a dollar is always a dollar") to the international arena by tying all national currency units firmly to either gold or the dollar. However, the "joint" between national currencies and national price structures should not be rigid. It should be supple and vary with discrepancies of national inflationary trends (the so-called purchasing-power parities).

The basic argument for fixed parities as policy instruments was that, combined with limited international liquidity reserves, fixed parities would help integrate national monetary policies. The deficit country would be forced into contraction, the surplus country prodded into expansion. The argument was reasonable as long as these reactions to changing reserves were considered desirable, possible, and probable. Even then, it was obvious, however, that the fixing of par values had to be accompanied by the artificial manipulation of another price of strategic importance – the discount rate.

Once the fixed-rate system is no longer permitted to produce these effects, once it is losing its power to bring about external balance and to maintain currency convertibility, fixed parities should no longer be maintained for their own sake.

The present international payments system does not rest on permanently fixed par values. The members of the International Monetary Fund are permitted to change the par values of their currencies if the Fund is satisfied "that the change is necessary to correct a fundamental disequilibrium."

Once parity adjustments are permissible, most arguments for fixed par values collapse: long-run transactions no longer rest on the safe foundation of a stable international value of the currency unit; monetary and fiscal policies are no longer forced to defend international liquidity reserves through inconvenient domestic policies; and harmonization of national policies can no longer be counted on, with the result that needed adjustments are brought about belatedly and abruptly through substantial devaluations and upvaluations. Emphasis in recent years on liquidity rather than adjustment indicates the increasing erosion of the very discipline on which the advocates of fixed exchange rates try to rest their case.

These ill-effects of the adjustable-peg system are now rather generally admitted, but have led some policy-makers to the wrong conclusion that par-value changes must be avoided at all cost – even at the cost of negating the real meaning of the whole system through the introduction of more and more stringent controls.

So much for an analysis of the magic triangle. Now to the question of how we can break out of this bad combination of interdependent limiting forces.

Flexible Exchange Rates

It should not be necessary to state the case for flexible exchange rates in market economies whose very logic depends on price reactions to changes in demand and supply. Nevertheless, this particular price, the rate of exchange, enjoys the unique distinction of being the only price that is kept artificially fixed with the approval of businessmen and bankers, and the support of many economists.

The main arguments against exchange-rate flexibility are well known: flexible rates, we are told, add new and additional risks to international transactions, foster speculation, and are an invitation to disregard the balance-of-payments implications of national economic policies. Robert Triffin, for instance, accuses the advocates of flexible rates of making the exaggerated claim that "fluctuating exchange rates would automatically equalize cost disparities which derive from diverging national monetary policies, so that every country would be free to follow the most contradictory paths, without disturbing in the slightest the international payments equilibrium."[1] Exchange-rate flexibility seems, somehow, to convey the notion of self-aggravating depreciation, extremely wide fluctuations, or an irresistible urge to practice competitive depreciation. It is taken for granted that to stray from the virtuous path of fixed exchange rates would mean the end both of national monetary discipline and international cooperation.

This view is much too pessimistic. The exchange-rate variations needed for the achievement of external equilibrium may be quite modest. A system with flexible exchange rates does not, like the present system, postpone the adjustment process and is therefore likely to avoid the development of discrepancies which under fixed rates will eventually call for major adjustments of par values or for exchange controls. That countries would not pay attention to their external balances, as Triffin suggests, is as unlikely as complete neglect of domestic policy aims under fixed rates; nor would floating rates be an invitation to competitive exchange depreciation. When market forces are permitted to operate, competitive depreciation cannot exist. Sustained undervaluation can only occur under the present adjustable-peg system.

However, notwithstanding these arguments in favor of flexible exchange rates, most practitioners and some academic economists believe that complete freedom for exchange-rate variations would mean the end of monetary discipline, that exchange rates would fluctuate wildly and that, far from producing external balance, the system would be injurious to international trade relations and capital flows. Whether right or wrong, these beliefs are too firmly ingrained to permit serious practical consideration of a system of freely floating exchange rates. The question arises, therefore, whether, if not full, at least greater exchange-rate flexibility could be introduced.

[1] Robert Triffin, "Die Währungsordnung des XX. Jahrhunderts" in *Inflation und Währungsordnung* (Erlenbach-Zürich und Stuttgart: Eugen Rentsch Verlag, 1963), p. 149.

A move to greater exchange-rate flexibility implies that the present system already contains some elements of flexibility. There are, indeed, two such elements. One is the permission of fluctuations of exchange rates around par values within a very narrow range; the other is the already mentioned adjustable-peg feature of the Bretton Woods arrangements.

Increased flexibility can be created by widening the margins of permissible exchange-rate variations from the present 1 percent on either side of parity to, say, 2-1/2 or 5 percent. This method of adding flexibility to a fixed par-value system was practiced even under the old gold standard[2] and was strongly recommended by J.M. Keynes in his *Treatise on Money*.[3] It is now often referred to as the band proposal, the "band" marking the total range, up and down, over which the rates are permitted to fluctuate. Official sales and purchases of foreign exchange would become obligatory and automatic as soon as the intervention points are reached. Official purchases of foreign exchange would prevent the value of foreign currencies from dropping below the intervention point. Official sales out of reserves would prevent an appreciation of the foreign currencies beyond the upper limit.

In the eyes of advocates of exchange-rate flexibility, the widened band would offer a solution only if the permitted exchange-rate variations were able to handle the adjustment problems which are created by diverging national economic policies (or by excessively large unilateral payments) *within* the band. If the band is not wide enough and the adjustment effects are too weak, if national divergencies do not reverse themselves (or unilateral transfers remain excessive), the exchange rates will get stuck at the support points. This would indicate that the widened band did not offer enough flexibility and that a change of par-values would have to take place.

In this case, the system would seem to be once more exposed to all the weaknesses of the adjustable peg. However, par-value changes do not have to be of the type that became characteristic for the first quarter-century of Fund operations. Small and frequent parity changes (crawling, sliding, or gliding parities) can be substituted for the present practice of discrete and large adjustments of the peg.

[2] See Jacob Viner, *Studies in the Theory of International Trade* (New York: Harper and Brothers, 1937), pp. 206-207; Arthur I. Bloomfield, *Monetary Policy under the International Gold Standard: 1880-1914* (Federal Reserve Bank of New York, 1959), p. 52.

[3] John Maynard Keynes, *A Treatise on Money*, Vol. 2 (New York: Harcourt, Brace and Company, 1933), chapter 36.

The two moves toward greater exchange-rate flexibility do not conflict. A combination of the widened band and the gliding peg can be referred to as a movable band.

The Band Proposal

The band proposal is a compromise which can be interpreted either as a very limited system of floating rates or as a fixed par-value system with widened gold points. In the words of Robert V. Roosa, market forces are permitted to "demonstrate the basic strength or weakness of a currency", and price reactions give "sensitive signals of changes in fundamental forces." Nevertheless predetermined limitations for these price fluctuations maintain "fixed points of reference" and prevent the degeneration of foreign exchange markets into "disorderly chaos."[4]

Whether this compromise favors discipline or freedom depends on the chosen width of the band in conjunction with the supply of international liquidity reserves. Small reserves combined with a broad band can have about the same effect as a narrow band with very large reserves. It would not be correct, therefore, to say that a widening of the band will weaken discipline. Changes in international liquidity reserves, furthermore, would no longer be the only gauge by which to judge the international position of a currency. "After all, exchange-rate movements are very clear and loud warning signals. They are much more noticeable by the public than are reserve movements."[5] Even a substantial widening of the band, therefore, need not be resisted on the grounds that this would be bad for monetary discipline.

If international liquidity reserves and widened bands are considered as trade-offs, the latter have the advantage that exchange-rate variations produce real adjustments while larger reserves only help postpone adjustments. The proper choice depends on the nature of the imbalances that are to be corrected. Temporary imbalances should be financed out of liquidity reserves; more deep-seated disequilibria should be eliminated.

[4]See Robert V. Roosa, "The Beginning of a Policy" and "Banking and the Balance of Payments" both in *Factors Affecting the United States Balance of Payments* (Joint Economic Committee, 1962), pp. 328 and 339; *Monetary Reform of the World Economy* (New York and Evanston: Harper and Row, 1965), p. 27.

[5]William Fellner in *Maintaining and Restoring Balance in International Payments*, ed. by William Fellner, Fritz Machlup, and Robert Triffin (Princeton, N.J.: Princeton University Press, 1966), p. 122.

The adjustment of the trade balance through exchange-rate variations takes time but its start is instant and automatic. The needed
corrections are not postponed for years as under the fixed par-value
system with a very narrow band. The time lag in the adjustment
process will let exchange rates move beyond the long-run equilibrium
point for the now existing market conditions. Lundberg[6] and
Meade[7] have pointed out that these temporary deviations will induce
private speculation to move funds from the surplus into the deficit
currency in expectation of a rebound once the real adjustment has
been accomplished. Private speculative capital will thus finance
temporary imbalances and prevent an overreaction of trade adjustments where no serious disequilibrium is involved.

Experience has shown that fixed exchange rates produce disequilibrating capital movements in dilemma cases: the surplus country
with the high employment level tries to check domestic inflation and
thereby attracts funds from the deficit country that follows expansionist policies to combat recession.

A system permitting increased exchange-rate flexibility within a
wider band would help restrain the disequilibrating capital flow
certain to be generated under fixed parities. As in the case of fixed
rates, the interest rate would be low in deficit country D, to increase
employment, and high in surplus country S, to stop inflation. The
interest-rate differential, therefore, would still tend to guide the
international flow of private short-term capital in the wrong direction. But in a system with exchange-rate flexibility exchange-rate
variations would tend to counterbalance the interest-rate differential.
The exchange-rate of S-currency would appreciate, the rate of
D-currency would depreciate, and these changes in exchange rates
would reduce, compensate, or overcompensate the profit to be
derived from the interest differential. Disequilibrating capital flows
from low-interest country D to high-interest country S would be

---

[6] Erik Lundberg in *Skandinaviska Banken Quarterly Review*, October 1954.

[7] James E. Meade in "The Future of International Payments" in *Factors Affecting the
United States Balance of Payments* (Joint Economic Committee, 1962).

[8] The case in which the deficit country enjoys full employment and the surplus country
suffers from unemployment is regarded as a non-dilemma case, because economic policies
aiming at external and internal balance need not conflict. The deficit country with full
employment can be expected to have high interest rates because of its high level of
economic activity, and it may raise these rates in an attempt to combat domestic inflation
and to attract short-term foreign funds to eliminate the deficit. The surplus country, by
contrast, tries to stimulate economic activity through low interest rates, thereby encouraging an outflow of short-term capital that, owing to the country's surplus position, would
create no problems. In a system with fixed exchange rates, the changing differentials in

reduced, stopped, or even reversed by the exchange-rate differential that grows with each additional capital transfer. In other words, market forces would take care of the situation.[8]

Choices

The band proposal offers a number of choices, and it will be necessary to find out which arrangements will be best.

(1) It might be advisable to widen the band gradually as those engaged in foreign transactions gain confidence in the new system. However, this gradual approach would presuppose a general realignment of exchange rates since otherwise some rates would immediately get stuck at the support points.

(2) It has been argued that one and the same band cannot be equally well suited for trade transactions and capital movements and that, for instance, a band capable of adjusting exports and imports would be too wide for capital transactions in international financial centers. However, since it is impossible to charge different prices for different uses of a completely fungible market object, all that can be said is that the individual countries must make their choice in their own best interest.

(3) It must be decided whether central banks are to intervene inside the band or to limit their intervention to purchases or sales at the support points. Since these transactions are not likely to be delayed to the very last moment when the support points are actually reached, it could easily be that the band would be composed of an inner band of non-intervention plus outer rims in which interventions would normally take place.

(4) Since international capital movements are induced by interest-rate differentials and by exchange-rate variations, central banks may

interest rates between deficit and surplus countries are expected to help adjust national price levels and the trade balance, while the induced international flow of short-term capital helps finance the deficit until the adjustment is completed. Even under the old gold standard the interest-rate differentials were supported by the small exchange-rate variations between the gold points. The exchange rate of the deficit country D would depreciate temporarily and make it more attractive for speculators in surplus country S to purchase D-currency, enjoy temporarily the higher interest rate in D, and repurchase S-currency after equilibrium has been achieved and D-currency has returned to parity. A widening of the band would strengthen these equilibrating short-term capital movements. The capital flows induced by exchange-rate variations alone might even be strong enough to provide the needed foreign funds to finance the temporary external imbalance and give the monetary authorities the opportunity of handling interest-rate changes with greater consideration of the requirements of internal equilibrium.

want to add exchange-rate manipulation inside the band to their arsenal of monetary instruments.

(5) Several writers[9] have suggested an asymmetrical band that would stress appreciations of surplus currencies more than deprecia-tions of deficit currencies. For example, the upper margin would be 3 percent while the lower margin would stay at the present figure of one percent. This arrangement would force the surplus countries with undervalued currencies to make a greater contribution to international balance than the deficit countries with overvalued currencies and, thereby, build an anti-inflationist feature into the system.

(6) Many advocates of the widened band want to combine it with a gliding parity. This combination, the crawling or gliding band or band and crawl, can be recommended, unless we are afraid that the simultaneous use of band and crawl would seriously weaken the firm guidance for national monetary policies which may possibly be gained from a band with absolutely fixed support points.

Band and Crawl

Of course, the widened band will not achieve its purpose if the disequilibrating forces of diverging national monetary policies exceed the equilibrating power of exchange-rate variations inside the band. Once the exchange rates become stuck at the support points, the system has again turned rigid. Flexibility can then be maintained by moving the parity in very small and relatively frequent instalments and by not more than, say, 2 percent per year.

Harry G. Johnson argues, that for those persuaded of the case for flexible rates, the crawling peg is definitely to be preferred to the wider band because the latter would provide only a once-for-all increase in the degree of freedom of exchange rates to adjust to changing circumstances.[10] However, the question need not be which of the two instruments for greater flexibility we *prefer*, the band or the crawl. There is no need to choose. In all probability both band and crawl will be used, and in this cooperation of band and crawl, the band is more important than Harry G. Johnson suggests.

[9] For instance George H. Chittenden, William Fellner, Fritz Machlup, and Robert V. Roosa in *Approaches to Greater Flexibility of Exchange Rates, The Bürgenstock Papers,* Arranged by C. Fred Bergsten, George N. Halm, Fritz Machlup, and Robert V. Roosa, Edited by George N. Halm (Princeton, N.J.: Princeton University Press, 1970)

[10] Harry G. Johnson, "The Case for Flexible Exchange Rates, 1969" in *Approaches to Greater Flexibility of Exchange Rates,* op. cit., pp. 107-108.

In overemphasizing the crawl we underestimate the equilibrating power of the widened band. We should not be unduly impressed by the divergencies of national monetary policies as they exist today. These divergencies were in part produced, and certainly exaggerated, by overvaluations and undervaluations as they are maintained under the adjustable-peg system. The postponement of adjustments has made things increasingly worse. We had, in fact, a system which led to *mal*adjustments. The maintenance of wrong exchange rates pried the monetary policies of the member countries further apart by enhancing both inflationary and deflationary trends. Surplus countries with undervalued currencies exposed themselves to added inflationist pressure while deficit countries, not willing to interrupt national economic expansion for reasons of external balance, went deeper and deeper into deficit. These developments could not have happened to the degree in which they did occur, had flexible rates within a widened band been permitted to help balance the external accounts. It is wrong, therefore, to base estimates on the needed degree of exchange-rate variations or parity changes on the experiences of the more recent past.

If we want to be pessimistic about the future divergencies of national monetary policies and the integrating power of exchange-rate variations inside a widened band, we shall also have to ask whether even a crawl of not more than 2 percent per year will be enough and whether a faster crawl could solve the problem of disequilibrating speculation which will inevitably be connected with substantial parity changes.

Nothing argues against a combination of band and crawl. Both rest on the same criticism of the present system and both will provide more flexibility. It makes sense to add the crawl to the widened band when we assume that unidirectional deviations of national monetary policies may eventually exceed the adjustment capabilities of the band. For the same reason, it makes sense to consider the widened band the first step on the road to greater flexibility and the gliding peg the second step.

The crawl does not one-sidedly aid the band. The band may be able to aid the crawl. It can provide guidance for the practical operation of a gliding-peg system. For this operation, it will be essential to gauge the degree of the existing external imbalance which calls for the shifting of the parity. Variations of exchange rates within a widened band may offer the most reliable evidence. Furthermore, if the band is relatively wide in comparison with the permitted yearly crawl (say, 6 percent against 2 percent), the parity adjustments can take place, as it were, *inside* the band and thus become invisible. This point is important in view of the difficulties that may be caused by private speculation.

In deciding on the relative importance of band and crawl, we should not forget that the widened band permits market forces to operate while the crawling-peg arrangement deals with a difficult question of price-setting. If we interpret the trend toward limited exchange-rate flexibility as a partial return to the operational procedures of a market economy, the band is more attractive than the crawl, and we may conclude that the crawl should not be stressed at the expense of the band.

Band, Crawl, and the Dollar[11]

Playing the role of international money (transaction and inter-vention currency) and unit of account (common denominator or numéraire), the dollar also finds itself in a special position with respect to the band and crawl proposals. When we assume a band of a total width of 10 percent, currencies *A* and *B* can be as far as 10 percent apart. However, the dollar, as common denominator, can differ from any one of the other currencies by not more than 5 percent or one-half of the total band.

The widened band, therefore, would not apply to the United States in the same manner as to all the other members of the system and would continue the asymmetry of the payments system which is connected with the role of the dollar as intervention currency and numeraire. In today's adjustable-peg system all members of the International Monetary Fund except the United States enjoy the potential safety-valve of parity changes if they find themselves in fundamental disequilibrium. Under the wider band, the adjustment possibilities via exchange-rate variations would be limited to one-half of those open to other Fund members. As a matter of fact, the dollar rate would not be determined by the policy of the United States but by the sum of the decisions of all other countries concerning their position to the dollar.

Should the United States nevertheless welcome the widened band?

An affirmative answer would have to consider that the present

[11] See C. Fred Bergsten's paper "The United States and Greater Flexibility of Exchange Rates" in *Approaches to Greater Flexibility of Exchange Rates*, op. cit., pp. 61-75.

situation of the United States also implies certain advantages. The role of the dollar as reserve currency means that all surplus countries stand ready to buy dollars in unlimited amounts when an oversupply of dollars must be taken off the market to prevent an appreciation of surplus currencies. This means automatic financing of payments deficits of the United States. If the band for permissible exchange-rate variations is widened while the dollar is still used as reserve currency, the effect on the United States will be in the nature of a compromise. The regular advantage of the widened band, that is, its beneficial adjustment effects on trade and capital flows, would be limited to one-half of the potential maximum effect for other countries; but to the extent that surplus countries would have to buy dollars at the margin, they would still finance a remaining deficit of the United States. A quasi-automatic supply of liquidity for the reserve-currency country compensates for the more limited elbow-room for exchange-rate adjustments.

Technical difficulties could arise if the band were widened while the gold value of the dollar remained relatively fixed as at present. The dollar could depreciate and appreciate in terms of other currencies by as much as 5 percent, but in terms of gold by only 1 percent. Accordingly, it would seem that central bankers would prefer gold to the dollar as the safer reserve asset or that, in the case of an expected dollar depreciation, they would move into gold and, in the case of a dollar appreciation into dollars. However, we ought to be able to assume that considerations other than mere security and profitability would prevail at official levels.

Not a Panacea

The band-crawl proposals do not solve all problems of the world's monetary system. The problems of liquidity and confidence remain but will become less acute as soon as a real adjustment process via exchange-rate and parity changes will be permitted to work. The demand for international liquidity will not disappear as it would under freely floating rates, but it will become more manageable; and, as adjustment and liquidity are better handled than before, confidence in the system will improve.

In the end, however, all international monetary systems can be expected to work only if national monetary policies are reasonable. We cannot argue that a system composed of the elements of convertibility, limited flexibility, and widely diverging national inflationist trends can be made to function. On the other hand, it is difficult to see why exchange-rate variations should not be as good a disciplinarian as changes in liquidity reserves and why international monetary cooperation and multilateral surveillance could not be applied to the administrative problems of band and crawl.

DISCUSSION

RICHARD E. CAVES

I am happy to be able to say at the start that I am in agreement with the great bulk of George Halm's paper. That is quite fortunate, since he is agreeable to so many alternative proposals to the present system that he becomes invulnerable to attack on any one in particular. He will accept both band and crawl; indeed, the limits of his band behave like the U.S. national debt ceiling, changing with only moderate inconvenience before they threaten to constrain the actual state of affairs. Furthermore, I gather that, if anyone gave him his preferences and made central bankers putty in his hands, he would have completely flexible exchange rates. In any case, always being an admirer of flexibility, I will not try to pick out any variant of this proposal and identify it as the Halm plan, but I shall comment rather on the relationship among several aspects of proposals that make use of the band device.

I would like first of all to reflect for a moment on the nature of the diagnoses that lead people either toward a crawling peg, as an alternative to the present adjustable peg, or toward a band proposal (which I'll define as a band with limits that do not change except perhaps in discrete steps). These two proposals stem from rather different diagnoses of what is allegedly wrong with the adjustable peg system employed under the Bretton Woods Agreement. The crawling peg is being supported by those who are concerned primarily with getting exchange rates changed in a more orderly fashion than they have been, and permitting these changes to proceed far enough to restore equilibrium. They are concerned simply with altering exchange rates and not with what one might call the policy system of the fixed exchange rate — its impact on the leverage of domestic policy instruments, speculative capital flows and the like.

Supporters of the band proposal, on the other hand, come to it from quite a different diagnosis of what is wrong with the adjustable peg system. They are worried primarily over the consequences of the policy system that results from fixing the exchange rate (or changing it by discrete jumps). They may fear the volume of speculative capital flows when people expect a rate change, or the government restrictions that may be imposed on commercial transactions in attempts to defend a fixed parity. Supporters of the band proposal

135

may also worry about the impact of the fixed exchange rate on the leverages of domestic economic policy or on the relative adequacy of the number of the policy instruments. Finally, they may fear that the adjustable peg will adjust by inappropriate amounts.

In short, quite different diagnoses of the ills of the adjustable peg system are made by those who would opt for the crawl, and those who would opt for the band. Those who like the crawl implicitly like fixed exchange rates, but want to get them changed a little more neatly. Those who like the band implicitly like the floating exchange-rate system and the impact that it has on the operation of economic policy; but they are concerned about having some ultimate limits on the movement of speculative capital and its impact on actual exchange rates. In short, you might say the band proposal appeals to nervous floaters and the crawl to nervous supporters of the fixed exchange rate.

Effects of the Band on Domestic Economic Policy

Most of my comments about the band proposal will be related to its effect as an exchange-rate system on the use of domestic economic policy. This topic has received less attention in our discussions here than the other aspects of adjustment mechanisms, and I will argue that there is an important problem about the impact of the band proposal on the leverages of domestic economic policy instruments. Professor Halm mentions a familiar proposition from the theory of economic policy: given two policy objectives – domestic stability and foreign-exchange equilibrium under a fixed rate – and two policy instruments – monetary and fiscal policy (excluding exchange-rate variation) – then you may be able to set the two policies simultaneously so as to achieve both goals. He is quite skeptical about this, citing the fungibility of money as one reason why it won't work. I don't follow that objection, since the logic of the proposition requires only that the relative leverage of monetary policy on domestic equilibrium and the foreign balance be different from that of fiscal policy on the domestic and foreign balances. In principle, if the leverages are different, some combination can be found that will make it all work out. If one objects to this on the ground that it requires excessive finesse in quantification, timing, and the badgering of Congress, however, I would agree.

In any case, if concern arises over the number of policy instruments or their flexibility for dealing with the set of policy targets arising with a fixed exchange-rate system — whether permanently fixed, adjustable, or a crawling-peg system — then one may very well be attracted either to a band or a totally flexible exchange-rate regime. I agree with Professor Halm that the flexible rate does save one policy instrument. This argument is not accepted by everyone, specifically not by Professor Kindleberger. It thus merits a closer look.

Two sorts of argument are made against this familiar proposition that the flexible exchange rate removes one policy target. The first is that central bankers in fact won't let the rate alone. I personally have never heard a central banker say that, only economists without obvious access to classified information. Even if central bankers did take this position, it might call not for fixed rates but rather for a treaty binding them to leave the flexible exchange rate alone. Sometimes the argument goes farther to insist that pressure groups will force governments to intervene in the exchange market for their benefit. To take a simple form of the argument, exporters expect that their activities will be more profitable if the exchange rate is depreciated and will hector the government to lower the rate for their benefit. Is this a major threat to the use of any kind of exchange flexibility — whether band or total? Professor Halm and I both doubt it, and I would like to suggest a reason or two.

Consider what would have to be done to favor the export interests. The government must incur a budgetary cost — that is, to lay out its own currency to buy up foreign exchange — to lower the value of its currency on the market. It can be shown that the cost of giving exporters a little thrill by this device is greater than would be the subsidy-equivalent value of the benefit to them. (The political processes admittedly do not always pick the most efficient means of helping out various interest groups.) Furthermore, outlays must be continued period after period if favoritism for exporters is to continue; a one-shot attack on the rate gives them only a one-shot benefit. The government must keep accumulating reserves, laying out its own currency, year after year in order to continue the game. In short, nobody can say that the political process will never force governments to meddle with ostensibly flexible exchange rates for purposes other than transitory stabilization, but such meddling is a costly and transitory way to achieve its assumed objectives.

The effect of adopting exchange-rate flexibility is not just to reduce the number of policy instruments needed. It also changes the leverages of economic policy instruments on domestic policy. We owe principally to Marcus Fleming and Robert Mundell the proposition that with capital internationally mobile in response to interest-rate differentials, the exchange-rate regime affects the impact on aggregate demand or employment of fiscal relative to monetary policy. A flexible exchange rate with a high degree of international capital mobility tends to make monetary policy relatively more effective for altering domestic aggregate demand, and fiscal policy relatively less, than a regime of fixed rates. Unlike the effect of flexibility in reducing the needed number of instruments, however, this change in the leverage of monetary and fiscal policy on the domestic target may or may not argue for flexibility in a particular case.

The Canadian Experience

To illustrate this, let me refer to the Canadian experience under the flexible exchange rate. Professor Kindleberger suggested last night that the policy failures that occurred in Canada in the late 1950's and early 1960's somehow show that the flexible exchange rate failed to work properly. Instead, this case reveals an error in the use of policy instruments of a type that could have occurred with any exchange-rate system. In the late 1950's, in conditions of relatively high unemployment and with a flexible exchange rate and highly mobile international capital flows, the Bank of Canada chose — for good or bad reasons of its own — to raise, not lower, the interest rate. In these conditions, the maneuver tended not only to discourage investment and reduce aggregate demand at home; it also sucked capital into the country, drove up the exchange rate and, in turn, lowered the rate of employment and raised the rate of unemployment by worsening the current-account balance.

This sort of unfortunate choice of policy could just as well have been made under a fixed-rate regime by a different but analogous mistake. If Canada had faced the same conditions except for having a fixed exchange rate, tightening rather than easing fiscal policy would have amounted to an analogous mistake. Not only would a tightening of fiscal policy obviously have an unfortunate direct impact on employment, it also would have tended to remove securities from domestic portfolios as the government's net deficit fell (or its net surplus rose), thus reducing the supply of assets in Canadian portfolios relative to the level of private expenditure. That ratio would have been readjusted either through a contraction of expenditure or a recoupment purchase of securities abroad. These forces would have also created a two-edged tendency to reduce further the level of unemployment. In short, under either a fixed or a fluctuating exchange rate regime, there is always one way to make a spectacular blunder in economic policy. No one ever claimed, in my presence, that exchange flexibility guarantees against policy mistakes.

Speculative Capital Flows under the Band Proposal

One reason I wanted to introduce this discussion of the problem of policy leverages is it raises one question about the band proposal that has not generally been considered. Resting as it does on a presumption of a range of exchange-rate flexibility bounded by a floor and a ceiling, the band proposal obviously has important implications for speculative capital flows. In fact one can predict alternative effects of the band proposal on speculative flows, and I only want to lay out the possibilities rather than proclaim one of them as most likely. On the one hand, if people really believe that the government has adequate reserves and determination to defend the band limits, then the band might have the following effect on speculative capital flows: when the rate lies somewhere well within the limits, speculation might at times be destabilizing, tending to push it towards one limit or the other. But, as the rate approaches the limit, speculators may expect that the government will hold at the limit. As the rate approaches the lower limit, speculation would become entirely one-way and operate in a stabilizing direction with regard to the overall band.

Another interpretation is possible. If the rate has been floating well within the band, people might conjecture that it is going to stay somewhere in the middle, and exchange speculation might be stabilizing when the rate is near the middle of the band. On the other hand, as it approaches the edges of the band, especially the lower edge, people might conjecture that the floor cannot be held, and speculation might work adversely. In short, one can make opposite arguments about the effect of exchange-rate speculation at different points within the band or at the limits. The point that I want to make for further development is only that the behavior of exchange-rate speculation is presumptively not homogeneous within various parts of the band.

I shall argue next that the behavior of exchange speculation has an important impact on those leverages of domestic policy instruments analyzed earlier. This is, I think, a rather important theoretical point that has not been developed in the published literature. Consider the example I gave you earlier. As a country moves from a pure fixed to a pure flexible exchange-rate regime, theory predicts that fiscal policy is replaced by monetary policy as an effective way of changing domestic aggregate demand or employment. What about the infusion of exchange-rate-sensitive — that is, speculative — capital flows into this model? Insofar as exchange speculation under a floating-rate regime stabilizes the exchange rate, the private speculators are behaving to some extent the same way the government does when it defends a fixed rate. Stabilizing speculation tends to shift the relative leverage of fiscal and monetary policy somewhere between what it would be with a pure fixed exchange rate regime and with a theoretical flexible exchange rate regime with no speculative capital flows — stabilizing or adverse. On the other hand, if destabilizing speculation does occur — although the case is uninteresting, because one is then off and away — it would push the relative policy leverage, as it were, beyond the point reached under the pure flexible exchange rate system with no speculative flows. This would involve a further augmentation of the relative effectiveness of monetary as against fiscal policy for maintaining domestic equilibrium.

I hope now I can bring together this rather complicated line of argument. I suggested, first, that exchange speculation is not homogeneous within the limits of the band and at these limits. It can vary with the rate's position within the band. Secondly, whether speculative behavior is stabilizing or destabilizing, and how much it is, will affect the leverage of domestic policy. My conclusion from those two propositions is that with the band proposal in force it would be difficult or impossible to predict what would be the leverage of domestic economic policy instruments. The responsiveness of capital flows to small changes in the exchange rate would be unpredictable or, at the very best, different depending on where you are within the band or at its limits. This I think is an important theoretical property of the band proposal. It certainly does not cause me to retreat to the adjustable-peg position, but rather confirms my leanings toward the flexible exchange rate.

Flexing the International Monetary System: The Case for Gliding Parities

RICHARD N. COOPER

Dissatisfaction with the present international monetary system mounted steadily from the mid to the late sixties. In the two years preceding October 1969 it permitted five major currency crises, involving gold and most of the major trading currencies. Calls for reform became legion. Defenders of the present monetary system have pointed out that the world economy has performed spectacularly well during the past two decades, probably better than during any corresponding period of history, and that while the crises were unsettling, they were largely superficial and were prevented from penetrating into domestic economies, as financial crises usually did in the past. A system that has done so well, they argue, should not be scrapped, but rather should be operated as it was intended to be when drawn up at Bretton Woods a quarter of a century ago.

I will argue that the success of the world economy during the past two decades occurred to some extent in spite of the Bretton Woods system rather than because of it, but that the system may be made to work without drastically overhauling it.

The Bretton Woods System on Paper

Let me first recall very briefly the main features of our international payments system. On the financial side, these are embodied principally in Articles of Agreement of the International Monetary Fund, laid down at Bretton Woods in 1944. On the side of merchandise trade, ground rules are embodied in the General Agreement on Tariffs and Trade (GATT), dating from 1947. In essence, these two documents call for freedom of international payments for goods and services exchanged among countries, for low tariffs, for fixed and stable exchange rates, for non-discrimination among countries, and for the avoidance of direct control over foreign trade. Drawn up against the background of the 1930s, they are designed to

Mr. Cooper is Frank Altschul Professor of International Economics, Yale University, New Haven, Connecticut.

avoid beggar-thy-neighbor trade and exchange policies and at the same time to allow countries that degree of national autonomy in monetary and fiscal policies necessary to maintain full employment.

The rules did not extend to international capital movements. Against the background of the extremely disruptive movements of capital during the interwar period, British officials who co-authored the Bretton Woods Agreement were extremely doubtful about permitting private capital to move freely among countries. The IMF Articles of Agreement not only permit controls over capital movements, but actually require all participating countries to help enforce whatever capital controls other participating countries have imposed. At the same time, however, the dominant country of the postwar period, the United States, has always attached considerable importance to freedom of private capital movements, and other countries have increasingly accepted this objective as well. Moreover, it has become increasingly clear that in times of financial unrest no sharp distinction between trade and capital transactions is possible.

It was recognized that imbalances in international payments would develop under the Bretton Woods system. Temporary imbalances were to be financed, partly out of national reserves, partly by borrowing at a new institution, the International Monetary Fund. "Fundamental" imbalances — surpluses as well as deficits — were to be corrected through discrete adjustments in exchange rates, from one fixed level to another.

The difficulty in this distinction between temporary and fundamental imbalances is that by the time the need for a change in the exchange rate becomes known to those officials who must make the decision, it is also known to everyone else. Discrete changes in exchange rates offer windfall gains to those who can shift their assets from one currency to another in correct anticipation of a change. Currency speculation has grown markedly in total volume, to the point at which in May 1969 nearly four billion dollars flowed into Germany in the course of a week in anticipation of a revaluation of the German mark, and over one billion dollars on a single day. (Four billion dollars amounted to nearly one-quarter of the total German money supply.) Here the logic of proscription on capital movements comes clear. To the extent that capital movements may be *effectively* restrained, both the possibility for large private gain and the disruption of market tranquility generated by large speculative flows are greatly reduced.

Actual Performance of the Bretton Woods System

This, in brief, is the international payments system. If it is defective, why has the world economy fared so well? I believe there are two reasons. The first is that the Bretton Woods System did not come fully into force until around 1960. We did not *start* with this system right after the Second World War. It represented the objective, not the reality. International commerce was severely restricted in the late 1940s, and the Bretton Woods Agreement allowed for a five-year transition period. The transition lasted nearly three times that long, and during the transition a process of *differential* trade liberalization provided a de facto balance of payments adjustment mechanism that was absent in theory. Early in the period, European and other countries discriminated heavily against American and Canadian goods, and to a lesser extent against goods from one another. As the payments positions of various European countries improved, they accelerated their trade liberalization. Those in payments difficulty slowed down the rate of liberalization and occasionally even reversed it. So long as restrictions on trade and other transactions could be relaxed differentially in accordance with balance-of-payments requirements, sources of imbalance could be corrected without frequent adjustments in exchange rates.

This process of differential trade and payments liberalization had largely run its course by the early sixties, but here a second unanticipated development obscured the underlying weaknesses of the adjustment process in the Bretton Woods System. I refer to the large U.S. payments deficits after 1958, which (when put on a consistent accounting basis) had their counterpart in the balance-of-payments surpluses elsewhere in the world. The reasons for the large U.S. deficits are controversial and need not detain us here. But their presence made the need for adjustment by other countries rather less pressing. In the absence of U.S. deficits, tensions between the French franc and the German mark, for example, would have occurred long before 1968. It is noteworthy that in 1968 the United States ran a balance of payments surplus, in a sense relevant for this discussion, for the first time since 1957, and an even larger surplus was run in 1969. These surpluses throw into relief tensions among other currencies that were earlier obscured by U.S. payments deficits. With the help of differential trade liberalization in the fifties and large U.S. payments deficits in the sixties, the Bretton Woods adjustment process was spared frequent or severe testing.

Somewhat paradoxically, the possibility of relying on U.S. payments deficits has also run its course, for other countries have become apprehensive about permitting the United States to spend abroad unchecked, whether it be for military adventures or for private foreign investment. Under the influence of European pressure and (unnecessarily) alarmist pronouncements by the U.S. financial community, American officials themselves became committed to elimination of the payments deficit.

So these two mitigating circumstances cannot be expected to persist into the future. In addition, however, there is a third complicating development. That is the sharp increase in the international mobility of capital. Under the influence of the revolution in communications and the vastly increased flow of information about the rest of the world, banks, firms, and individuals distinguish far less between domestic and foreign assets than they once did, and the erosion of this distinction is continuing. With increased awareness of investment opportunities abroad comes also increased awareness of the possibility for speculative gains on currency changes. The potential movements of funds in response to anticipated changes in exchange rates has become quite phenomenal. Potential movements are increased further, and the possibility for distinguishing in practice between transactions on current and capital account is further diminished, by the substantial growth of the multinational firm. Such firms can readily shift not only working balances but also commercial credits among their operations in different countries in such a way as to speculate in favor or against particular currencies. They may even adjust the commodity prices at which intrafirm transactions take place for the purpose of developing a long or short position in a particular currency.

Under these circumstances, reliance on discrete changes in exchange rates as the principal weapon for adjustment to fundamental payments imbalances becomes impracticable, for anticipated currency revaluation results in a transfer of public and national wealth (in the form of foreign exchange reserves) into private and usually foreign hands, while currency devaluation results in an arbitrary redistribution of wealth among private individuals and to a lesser (but increasing) extent will also transfer national wealth to foreigners. An additional deterrent is the fact that currency devaluation usually involves questions of national prestige and even the political fate of those with immediate responsibility.[1] Governments are reluctant to admit the failure implicit in a devaluation of the currency, and therefore procrastinate to the point at which devaluation cannot be avoided and currency speculation is correspondingly aggravated.

Not surprisingly, under these circumstances, countries have adopted a series of substitute measures, often violating the letter or the spirit of the postwar agreements, to keep their payments position under control but at the same time to avoid changes in currency parities. Most of the reversals in liberalization have involved capital movements, on which as noted above controls are technically permissible under the Bretton Woods Agreement. But countries have also engaged in extensive interference in foreign trade and services, resorting to a miscellany of ad hoc devices such as tying foreign aid, redirecting government procurement, selling arms, cutting embassy staffs, limiting foreign travel, et cetera. Canada (in 1962), Britain (in 1964), and France (in 1968) all imposed temporary measures directly interfering with private merchandise imports, in direct violation of their international commitments. Other countries have adjusted their tax systems in such a way as to encourage exports or to discourage imports. The Bretton Woods System also gives rise to considerable debate where the responsibility for certain imbalances lies, who should do what, who is not doing enough, and so on; it invites pretentious moralizing and contentious politicking, damaging to the international cooperation the system is supposed to foster.

The Bretton Woods payments system has become unworkable. We still do have exchange adjustments, such as the devaluation of sterling and other currencies in November 1967, but they almost always take place under *force majeure* rather than as an integral feature of a smoothly working adjustment mechanism.[2] To protect existing exchange parities, countries increasingly violate basic principles and purposes of the payments system. The absence of an

---

[1]In a sample of two dozen devaluing countries, mostly less developed countries, the probability that a Minister of Finance would lose his job within a year following a devaluation was increased three-fold over the corresponding experience of a control group. This illustrates the conflict between personal and national interest that may arise for the individuals responsible for framing national policy. See my "Currency Devaluation in Developing Countries: A Cross-Sectional Analysis," Gustav Ranis (ed.) *Government and Economic Development*, Yale Univ. Press (forthcoming).

[2]The French devaluation of August 1969 was an apparent exception, for the timing of the devaluation caught financial markets off guard; but most international firms and many individuals had already taken a short position in francs.

146   *The International* ADJUSTMENT MECHANISM

international adjustment mechanism will plague us increasingly in the seventies unless something is done about it. I see no escape from the choice between somewhat greater flexibility of exchange rates, on the one hand, or, on the other, more frequent resort to restrictions and other interferences with international transactions. Homilies about the need for countries to maintain tighter control over internal demand, even when they are to the point, are not likely to be received with grace or to be translated into action with the regularity and persistence required to avoid one or the other.

Compromise Solution: A "Gliding Parity" System

A possible compromise between the need for a long-term adjustment mechanism and a desire to preserve both a moderate degree of external "discipline" on domestic policies and pressures for international cooperation in framing economic policies resides in a scheme whereby exchange parities change slowly over time, but more or less automatically and in the direction required for payments adjustment. A system of "gliding parities" would provide a reasonable degree of certainty and stability in the short run, but would at the same time permit the gradual economic adjustments so necessary in the long run. In the remainder of this paper, I will argue for a particular version of the gliding parity proposal,[3] will indicate its merits and its limitations, and will compare it with alternative proposals for introducing greater exchange flexibility into the payments system.

Under this proposal, a country would be expected to change its exchange parity weekly whenever its payments position warranted a change. The weekly change in parity would be fixed at .05 percent, cumulating to about 2.6 percent a year if changes were made in the same direction every week. A change in parity would be triggered by a movement in the country's international reserve position. If reserves rose more than a stipulated amount during a given week, the country would announce at the end of the week an up-valuation in its parity for the following week, and vice versa for a decline in reserves. The movement in reserves would determine whether the parity changed or not, but not the amount of the change in parity, which

---

[3]This proposal is taken from my "Gliding Parities: A Proposal for Presumptive Rules," prepared for the Conference on Exchange Rates at Bürgenstock, Switzerland, in June 1969, and to be published in *Approaches to Greater Flexibility in Exchange Rates: The Bürgenstock Papers*, Princeton University Press, 1970.

would be fixed at .05 percent. Market exchange rates need not change by the full amount of the parity, however, for the country's central bank might adopt a strategy of supporting the market rates temporarily even after a change in parity.

Changes in parity would be presumptive rather than mandatory. Where special circumstances influenced reserve movements, a country might ignore the presumption that the parity should be changed. But a country that failed to alter its parity when an alteration was indicated would be required to explain and justify its decisions before other trading nations, which would meet on a regular basis several times each year to review international monetary developments. Any country that systematically ignored the presumptive rules and offered an unacceptable justification would be open to sanctions: for a country in deficit, no credit from the IMF and other international sources of balance-of-payments support; for a country in surplus, discriminatory "exchange equalization" duties against its products.

An arrangement such as this would provide relatively smooth accommodation to certain kinds of disturbance to balance-of-payments equilibrium. In particular, it would prevent or inhibit payments disequilibrium arising from:

1) gradual shifts in the patterns of demand, as incomes grow and tastes change, toward or away from the products of individual countries;
2) gradual changes in international competitiveness or other supply conditions, such as might arise from exhaustion of natural resources or from small differential rates of change in labor costs due in turn to different national choices regarding tolerable increases in money wages;
3) modest influences on trade positions due to alterations in national policies, such as changes in indirect tax rates and corresponding border tax adjustments.

This arrangement would not be well suited for coping with large disturbances to international payments, such as very large wage settlements or engagement in major overseas military adventures. For this reason large discrete changes in exchange parities, as called for under the Bretton Woods System, could not be ruled out. (The cumulative effects of small changes in parity might of course obviate some large parity changes that would otherwise be necessary.) The arrangement would offer somewhat greater scope, as compared with the present, for independent national monetary policies, but monetary conditions would still be subject to strong international influences, as they are today.

Effect on Trade and Capital Movements

Gliding parities would affect both trade and capital movements. The effect on trade would arise from the gradual change — upward or downward — in exchange rates, making goods and services in a country whose currency was appreciating less competitive than they otherwise would be, and the reverse for a country in deficit. In some cases these changes in exchange rates would merely neutralize opposite changes in other elements affecting competitiveness, for example small changes in wage costs or in border taxes, and thus would be preventive of changes in price competitiveness rather than corrective. In other cases they would produce compensatory changes in trade flows to offset disturbing changes in trade or other international transactions. In the latter cases, trade flows would have to be sufficiently sensitive to relative price movements for the system to work well. Empirical evidence suggests that the required degree of price sensitivity exists for most countries.

Influence on International Investment

Gradual changes in exchange parities would also influence long-term international investment, but the influence would be limited and, on balance, would mark an improvement as compared with the Bretton Woods system. Under fixed parities, portfolio capital may inappropriately flow to countries with high nominal interest rates resulting from inflationary pressures — at least until a change in parity is regarded as imminent. Under gliding parities, exchange depreciation and/or appreciation will offset such yield differences, without however, inhibiting long-term capital movements inspired by real, as opposed to nominal, differences in interest rates. Similarly, gliding parities would help to neutralize inappropriate incentives or disincentives to foreign direct investment based on divergent trends in money wage costs or certain national tax changes under (temporarily) fixed exchange rates while leaving uninhibited capital flows based on differences in real rates of return.

The impact of a gliding parity on short-term capital movements, hence its implications for monetary policy, is somewhat more complicated. The case in which gradual parity changes are widely expected must be distinguished from that in which the financial public is unsure whether parities will glide and, if so, in which direction. In the first case, monetary policy will have to be governed by balance-of-payments considerations if large outflows of interest-sensitive funds are to be avoided. In the second case, monetary policy will have somewhat greater scope than under the Bretton Woods system for devotion to domestic stabilization.

Strong and one-sided expectations about the direction in which the parity and actual exchange rates will move will be reflected in forward exchange rates. For example, a currency at its floor and expected to depreciate at the maximum rate would trade at a discount of at least 2-1/2 percent (annual rate) in the forward market vis-à-vis the intervention currency. Under these circumstances, strong interest arbitrage incentives would develop; and unless the country in question permitted its relevant interest rates to rise above those prevailing elsewhere by a corresponding amount, interest-sensitive capital outflows would ensue. In this respect, however, the gliding parity arrangement would not restrict the flexibility of monetary action any more than it is at present under similar circumstances.

Greater Scope for National Monetary Autonomy

On the other hand, if expectations about future exchange rate movements are diverse, a system of gliding parities would offer somewhat greater scope for national monetary autonomy than present arrangements. At present, a country whose exchange parity is not expected to change in the near future finds its flexibility to use monetary policy for domestic purposes increasingly circumscribed by a large and growing volume of interest-sensitive international capital.[4] While forward exchange rates are not technically pegged by official action, their movement is limited under these circumstances to a band hardly wider than the band officially allowable for spot exchange rates, for movements outside the spot floor and ceiling rates evoke speculative forward purchases or sales of the currency. The practical limits on forward exchange rate movements similarly limit deviations in domestic interest rates from those prevailing in major foreign financial markets, because deviations in excess of those permitted by the range of forward exchange rates would evoke

[4]Countries whose parities are expected to change also experience difficulty in preserving monetary autonomy, but for different reasons.

large-scale inward or outward movements of covered, interest-sensitive funds, thus weakening or even vitiating the intended effects of tight or easy monetary policy on the domestic economy.

Because under a gliding parity arrangement exchange rates could move in the course of a year by as much as 2.6 percent in either direction outside the band around parity, forward exchange rates could also range outside the initial band without evoking large, one-sided speculative forward purchases. To the extent that uncertainty prevailed about the direction and extent that the parity would glide, therefore, monetary policy would be given somewhat greater scope for pursuit of domestic objectives without being undercut by international capital movements.

A Case for Presumptive Rules for Parity Changes

It is tempting to make the rules governing changes in parity automatic and mandatory. Too often domestic politics and national prestige become involved in government decisions regarding exchange parities, and a fully discretionary system would very likely result in less frequent changes in parity than would be desirable. Even apart from the difficulty of devising automatic rules appropriate to all circumstances, however, governments as a practical matter are not likely to bind themselves to courses of action that they may not always conceive to be in their best interests. This difficulty can be resolved by laying down *presumptive rules,* of the type indicated in this proposal, which no country is obliged to follow, but which each country would be expected to follow in the absence of sound and persuasive reasons for not doing so. A procedure could be established in the International Monetary Fund or elsewhere for close and continuing examination by other member countries of those cases in which the presumptive rules were not followed.

Presumptive rules for parity changes must be based on some measure of balance-of-payments performance. Movements in reserves, spot exchange rates, and forward exchange rates all convey some information about a country's payments position. No single indicator will always be appropriate. However, simplicity is a virtue, and presumptive rules will be less seriously deficient if they are based on reserve movements tempered where necessary by other indicators on a discretionary basis, than if they are based on observed spot or forward rates. Forward rates may be held at a premium or discount by differences in national interest rates even when there is no net movement of funds, and such a premium or discount signifies nothing about a country's balance-of-payments position. A currency trading at a forward discount is not necessarily or even normally an over-valued currency.

An alternative version of gliding parities, the one most frequently discussed, would make the parity at each moment in time depend on some average of the spot exchange rates prevailing in the recent past. If the spot rate were below the parity, this would generally induce a fall in the parity; spot rates above parity would raise the parity. Under this scheme, the spot exchange rate is used as the key indicator of a country's payments position.

Two Difficulties

There are two difficulties with this proposal, apart from its automaticity, which has been discussed above. First, it neglects entirely the great importance of non-market transactions, such as the purchase of German marks for U.S. forces under NATO. Even when by agreement these transactions take place at market rates, they exert no direct pressure on the spot market since they occur outside the market. Thus a country's currency may be technically weak even when the country has a strong payments position, and vice versa. While conceivably this problem could be solved by requiring all foreign exchange transactions to go through the market, the parties involved would frequently object to such a stipulation, not only because of the transactions costs involved but also because of the influence that large purchasers could exert on the market. (U.S. official purchases of marks for use in Germany amount to nearly one billion dollars a year, for instance.)

Second, the authorities of a country might influence the movement of its parity by intervening in the exchange market, for example, by selling home currency to prevent appreciation, thereby thwarting the purposes of the scheme. To prevent this, it has been suggested that official market intervention within the exchange rate band must be prohibited. Apart from the fact that few governments are likely to agree to such a proscription, it will not solve the problem, for countries can influence market rates by other means, such as monetary policy.

Under the arrangement proposed here, in contrast, monetary authorities would be free, as now, to intervene in the exchange markets at times of their choosing. But they would have an incentive not to intervene within the band, since intervention (implying reserve movements) would presumptively require a change in parity in the direction which the authorities were resisting. Reserve sales to inhibit a fall in the market rate would call for a reduction of the parity, while purchases of foreign exchange to inhibit a rise in the rate would call for an increase in the parity. Any country that desires to maintain a constant exchange rate between its currency and some other currency can of course do so by following a monetary policy appropriate to that objective; its monetary policy then becomes fully dependent on conditions abroad, and monetary policy is truly (if one-sidedly) "coordinated," a necessary condition for a durable regime of fixed exchange rate without controls on international transactions.

There is, finally, some positive advantage in keying parity changes to reserve movements, since this would relate balance-of-payments adjustment explicitly to demands for reserves and would thereby highlight any national inconsistencies in the global demand for reserves. Under the Bretton Woods System, countries declare exchange parities but do not declare their demands for reserves, with the result that global demand may exceed global supply (or vice versa), and balance-of-payments adjustment policies may work at cross purposes as many countries attempt, unsuccessfully in the aggregate, to increase their reserves.[5] Under the presumptive rules proposed here, changes in parity would be keyed to national reserve changes relative to some normal, desired reserve increase. The declaration of desired reserve increases would, in turn, assure that the total demand for reserves matched the total supply — if necessary by adjusting the total supply (e.g. creation of SDRs).[6]

Transitional Problems

A difficulty with any new proposal is the transition during which it is put into effect, especially when the initial situation may be characterized, in this case, by large actual or suppressed imbalances in payments.

[5] Thanks to the reserve-currency role of the dollar and the relative indifference of the United States to its payments position, this problem was not acute during the fifties, since dollar outflows satisfied any residual demand for reserves in the rest of the world.

[6] Each country would thus have two reserve indicators under the scheme: (1) the target increase to allow for secular growth in reserves and (2) the amount by which reserve changes would have to exceed or fall short of this target increase before a change in parity was indicated.

It would be highly desirable with any innovation in the rules governing exchange rates to begin from a position of approximate payments equilibrium, at least among the major trading countries. As a practical matter, this may not be possible, even with some initial realignment of rates, since such changes may not be exactly right. Fortunately, however, transitional problems for a system of gliding parities are markedly less than for many other proposals regarding changes in the exchange rate regime. In particular, initial equilibrium, while desirable, is by no means a necessary precondition for the introduction of gliding parities.

Inaugurating the system from a position of disequilibrium would, for a time, assure the direction in which certain exchange parities would move; and this assurance, in turn, would provide incentive for speculating on currencies expected to rise in value and against those expected to fall. But this incentive would not necessarily be greater than that before the introduction of gliding parities in what is, by assumption, a position of widely recognized disequilibrium. The only new element is the certainty of parity change, but with that certainty also comes the certainty of small changes spread over a period of time (provided the new regime itself is credible) and the assurance of eventual correction (provided new sources of disequilibrium do not equal the corrective capacity of the parity changes). Moreover, the financial incentives of small changes in exchange rates can be compensated by corresponding differences in interest rates — lower on assets in an appreciating currency, higher on assets in a depreciating one. Thus, starting the arrangement in the presence of payments imbalances might require, at the outset, an adjustment in certain national interest rates to compensate for expected changes in parities. Since relative rather than absolute interest rates matter here, such an adjustment should be the subject of international discussion and agreement. Furthermore, where financial institutions maintain a rigid separation between capital and income on their accounts either by law or by accounting convention, some provision should be made for offsetting one against the other insofar as changes in capital valuation would result from changes in exchange parities.

Gliding Parities and Widened Band Proposals Compared

Before concluding, let me contrast this proposal for gliding parities with the proposal for introducing greater exchange flexibility by widening the band within which market exchange rates are free to fluctuate without required intervention by the monetary authorities. In my view, these two proposals serve basically different functions, and thus are complementary rather than competitive in their effects. So long as the exchange rate is within the band, wider bands introduce greater uncertainty with respect to the movement of exchange rates in the near future. As a consequence, a wider band permits greater national autonomy in the pursuit of monetary policy, for forward exchange rates are similarly free to move more widely than is true with a narrow band. Gliding parities permit somewhat greater monetary autonomy, but not so much as a much wider band would.

Second, a wider band would reduce the need for reserves to cover seasonal, cyclical, and other reversible balance of payments disturbances. These disturbances would be compensated by movements in market exchange rates, aided by stabilizing private speculation. To the extent that the parities remained credible, the need for international liquidity would be reduced.

A wider band would not permit adjustment to secular, or cumulative, disturbances to international payments, such as might arise from persistent divergences in national price or demand-for-import trends. These are the kinds of disturbance that a system of gliding parities is designed to accommodate. Once the floor or ceiling of a widened band is reached, a country would find itself in just the same condition as it does today under similar circumstances. Since I believe that such long-run divergences in balance-of-payments trends are inevitable, I cannot regard a widening of the bands as a permanent solution to the adjustment problem. It leaves us with all of the same problems outlined earlier in the paper. I find unpersuasive the claim that wider bands would make discrete parity changes easier. A market rate at the floor or ceiling of the widened band would certainly make the need for parity changes more obvious than it sometimes is today, but that need would be as obvious to private parties as to government officials, and would stimulate massive speculative flows of funds.

A widening of the bands is often linked with a proposal to permit parities to glide. However, it is not true, as has sometimes been claimed, that there is an organic connection between the width of the band and the permissible rate at which parities may glide. Under the proposal described earlier whereby the parity is linked automatically to an average of historical market rates, the band width, hence the possible deviation of actual market rates from the parity, obviously influences the rate at which the parity would glide. But when parity changes are keyed to reserve changes, a gliding parity is consistent with a variety of band widths; the two proposals are separable, and each can be considered on its merits.

Finally, I should add one tentative reservation about widening the bands or indeed any other proposal that might lead to substantial fluctuations in actual market exchange rates. Our understanding of the considerations which lead people to hold money is still highly imperfect. Ronald McKinnon has suggested that stability in purchasing power is an important consideration in the willingness to hold money and that, where the exchange rate of a currency fluctuates substantially against other currencies, residents may be tempted to move their holdings of cash balances from the fluctuating currency into a more stable one — a tendency that would increase in proportion to the importance of foreign goods in their expenditures.[7] Thus, stable currencies might "drive out" unstable ones, and evoke in turn national attempts to preserve national currencies through the use of controls to prevent flight into other currencies. Of course, as is frequently pointed out by the advocates of greater exchange flexibility, flexibility need not lead to instability. It need not, but it might; and therein lies the risk. This objection is not a serious one, however, for relations among major currencies.

While a system of gliding parities would be highly novel institutionally and, in that sense, would represent a sharp departure from present arrangements, its impact on trade and payments and on the need for close cooperation among major countries would be limited and, in that (more relevant) sense, it would represent a modest but possibly significant step in the evolution of the present international monetary system. Relations among currencies would be relatively stable, movements in exchange rates would be severely limited, pressures for coordination of national monetary and other policies would remain high, and movements in foreign exchange reserves — augmented when necessary by official borrowing from the IMF and elsewhere — would continue to absorb the bulk of swings in payments positions.

Within limits, however, a system of gliding parities would prevent the cumulative imbalances that arise from disparate national rates of

[7] R. I. McKinnon, "Optimal Currency Areas," *American Economic Review*, 53 (September 1963), pp. 717-24.

growth or disparate national rates of wage inflation, and by so doing it would reduce the need to resort to the import surcharges, tax devices to improve foreign receipts, and direct controls over international transactions that have once again become a common feature of the international economic landscape.

DISCUSSION

MARCUS FLEMING

Dick Cooper prefaced his excellent paper by taking a few pot-shots at the existing par value system set up at Bretton Woods. This has become a favorite sport wherever two or three economists are gathered together. I hold no particular brief for that system — perhaps I ought to as a Fund official — but recently, to my surprise, I have discovered in myself an impulse to rush chivalrously to its defense against what seem to me to be rather intemperate attacks and prophecies of doom. Dick admits in his paper that the period in which the Bretton Woods agreement and the GATT agreements have at least nominally prevailed has coincided with the period of unexampled prosperity and expansion in the world economy. Dick, however, would attribute this to rather special factors which have prevented the system from having its noxious effects. The special factors are the existence of discriminatory payments restrictions in the 1950's and the United States deficits in the 1960's. I would agree that the relaxation of anti-dollar discrimination was one of the factors that made the 1950's the success that it was, though I would remind you that it is very doubtful whether this development would have been possible without the devaluations of 1949. As for the U.S. deficits in the 1960's, these doubtless kept up the supply of world reserves and made it easier for countries other than the United States. At the same time the United States is part of the world, a fact which both the United States and the non-United States sometimes forget. Many of the symptoms of malaise that are pointed to by critics of the system really are things done by the United States. So that I think that the U.S. deficit has been at least a very ambiguous factor which may have helped the system in some respects but also harmed it in others. After all it is no very favorable sign if the central currency of the whole system is weak and under attack.

Reasons for Success of the World Economy in the Bretton Woods Period

I think that the reason for the success of the world economy during the Bretton Woods period is really much simpler, namely, the fact that countries by and large got their priorities right. They gave

Mr. Fleming is Deputy Director, Research Department, International Monetary Fund, Washington, D.C.

first priority to the maintenance of fairly full employment and reasonable internal stability (so far as these two things could be reconciled) and to the liberalization of trade, and were prepared in the last resort to adjust their exchange rates rather than sacrifice these primary values. Exchange adjustments may have come too late to prevent the spectacular crises that are always referred to, but they came in time to prevent any significant damage being done to world real incomes, and these after all are the primary objectives for which the Bretton Woods agreement was made. I would maintain that despite all its faults, the system has, to some extent, worked as it was originally intended to do.

Shortage of World Reserves

If the system has in recent years run into increasing difficulty, that is in my opinion entirely due to the increasing shortage of world reserves and reserve growth, combined with the increasing international mobility of capital. And as we know, steps have been taken — at first they were very improvised steps and later more systematic steps — to remedy the threatening shortage of world reserves. I certainly don't want to argue that the system is perfect, but I say that it ought to be judged not by comparing it with some textbook ideal, some concept of a perfectly competitive world economy, or even a perfectly operating, freely-flexible exchange rates system, but rather with the concrete available alternatives. Professor Cooper's paper is of course taken up with the examination of one such alternative — which the ill-mannered people have been accustomed to call the "crawling peg," but which I shall endeavor to refer to as the "gliding parity." I might say, before I go on, that I thought that Dick's particular variant of it was one of the most sophisticated and attractive versions that I had seen. Nevertheless, I feel that the faults that he found in the par value system and which, I agree, exist, are not really faults which the gliding parity system is particularly designed to correct. I would refer back to what Professor Caves said this morning — that many of the weaknesses in the present system would find a remedy rather in floating rates or in very wide margins within which rates can float, than in the particular device which we are discussing now.

Advantages of the "Gliding Parity" System

This doesn't mean that I am entirely unsusceptible to the general idea of the gliding parity. I am attracted by the general principle as a remedy for certain types of disequilibria, crawling disequilibria, that affect the current account balance of payments, whether these are due to differences of Phillips curves, differences in demand policies between countries, or structural factors. It is surely better that real adjustments should be avoided if they are unnecessary, and that necessary ones should be carried out gradually. And I agree that it would be very pleasant to be able to avoid the speculative consequences of delayed adjustment of the rates of exchange, and it would be nice to be able to avoid the excessive adjustment of rates of exchange which may sometimes take place when adjustment is too long delayed. A further advantage of the system of gliding parities, as compared to wider margins, is that it could conceivably apply to the United States. I don't think that Professor Cooper made this point, and I don't belong myself to the school of thought which believes that the par value of the dollar can never be changed, but I certainly think that the difficulties in changing it might be minimized if it were done by the gliding principle, rather than by discrete amounts.

Difficulties of Estimating Equilibrium Rates

On the other hand, any system of gliding parities is liable to run into difficulties because the factors affecting the balance of payments don't divide themselves conveniently into those that are clearly of a short-term character — and should therefore be financed — and those that are of a long-term character, gradually changing character, and should therefore be dealt with by means of a gliding parity. As regards the substantial abrupt changes of long-term equilibrium, such as have arisen from exceptional wage increases, Professor Cooper would admit that they necessitate the retention of possible discrete parity changes. Now that is a very important admission, because I think it has an influence on the way in which the whole system will operate. There are also changes of a cyclical or medium-term character, of the type that frequently affect capital flows. The capital flows in question may not be speculative; they are possibly quite normal capital flows; but they are essentially of a one-shot character. I have the impression that such flows are of increasing importance. If one thinks that such temporary shifts in the flows of funds should not be allowed to lead to flows of real resources and that exchange rates should not be affected by them, then the current behavior of market exchange rates provides very little guidance to the adjustment, gliding or otherwise, of exchange rates. Indeed, when such factors are important, it becomes very difficult to arrive at any firm estimate of the long-term equilibrium rate. I think that is the present case with respect to the dollar. The United States is presently in overall payments surplus and is nevertheless presumably in underlying deficit in the sense that over the long period it should have a more favorable current balance. In one sense it is in deficit and in another sense in surplus. One asks oneself, what over the long run would be the balance of payments of the United States if relative international price and cost levels remained unchanged? It is very difficult to say. It is very difficult in the case of Germany to say just how much the German mark is undervalued. So there is difficulty in determining what the correct rate is. On the other hand, if you think that such temporary flows of funds should lead to transfers of real resources, then gliding parities are surely inferior to floating rates or to wider margins as a means of achieving this.

This leads me on to what I think is the basic difficulty about implementing any system of gliding parities. The gliding parity has to move either in response to objective criteria, such as market rates of exchange or balance-of-payments deficits or surpluses, or at the discretion of national authorities (influenced, perhaps, to some extent by international authorities), or in response to some combination of these. Professor Cooper has devised a very interesting compromise formulation which combines the three. His device is one of presumptive rules that the country could persistently neglect only at the risk of some sort of international sanction.

Where the Gliding Is Done in Response to Automatic Criteria

I think it is easier to analyze the problem if one takes first the case where the gliding is done in response to automatic criteria, and then the case where it is purely discretionary, and finally the compromise solution. To the extent that the movement of the parity is automatically governed by statistical criteria, it may easily move in the wrong direction from the standpoint of long-term equilibrium, although admittedly by the very definition of long-term equilibrium, it must be moving in the right direction most of the time. Nevertheless, some of the time it will be moving in the wrong direction, or it may fail to move at all. For example, if a deficit is suppressed by restrictions on imports or capital exports, then the automatic indicator will fail to indicate and no move in the rate would take place.

From the standpoint of medium-term equilibrium, if you think the object is to keep countries in equilibrium in the medium term, the parity will usually move in the right direction, but the rate will attain appropriate levels only with a considerable time lag. If one adds the lag required for exchange rate changes to take effect on trade to the lag of the actual rate behind the balance-of-payments situation which gave rise to that rate, the ultimate effect on the current account will often be perverse even from a medium-term standpoint. I grant Professor Cooper that the automatic criterion on his scheme — the change in reserves — leads to a better reflection of the tendencies in the balance of payments, other than those generated by the government itself, than would a criterion based upon market exchange rates. However, even his criterion is not exempt from the faults mentioned above.

The Discretionary Form of the Gliding Parity

Now these faults are perhaps less important in themselves than in the excuse they give to national authorities to limit the scope of the automatic elements in the system. "You see," they will say, "how absurd it is to pay much attention to the weekly balance of payments, which may go in quite the wrong direction." In many cases that have been pointed to in the course of this conference, the contemporary balance of payments would have been a very poor guide to the direction in which long-term equilibrium lies. I would consider this result unfortunate because I happen to believe that the discretionary form of the gliding parity, however politically inevitable it is, is likely to work out even less well than the more automatic forms. To the extent that the gliding parity operates on the basis of government decree or the decisions of the monetary authorities, I believe that owing to its effect on capital flows it will normally increase the overall deficits of countries of overvalued currencies and the overall surpluses of countries of undervalued currencies. In the special case in which the country's temporary balance of payments is the contrary of its underlying positions this may be equilibrating but in the general case the effects will be disequilibrating.

My reasons for arriving at this conclusion are the following. If a government makes a decision, or if it consents to a small change in its parity, this is likely to be taken by the market as evidence that the authorities consider the rate to be significantly out of line. Governments are quite unable to detect, and even if they could detect, are unable to admit to, divergencies from equilibrium until these are significantly large. There will therefore be a high probability of continued small rate changes in the same direction and some remaining possibility of a large discrete change; the market will know that countries have not given up the right to make a big change. They will know that the authorities think there is something wrong with the rate or they wouldn't agree to the small changes. They know, therefore, that if speculation develops sufficiently, the government may be forced into the larger change.

I think this combination of circumstances is one which would lead to even greater disequilibrating speculation than under the present system. I think the combination of high probability of moderate profit and a chance of a big profit is just the kind of probability distribution of potential capital gains which is calculated to attract into the foreign exchange market a whole new stratum of speculative investors. I would expect exchange speculation effects to begin earlier in relation to any underlying disequilibrium and to be larger in cumulative amount than at present. But I would grant that the extreme crises might be less extreme since one would expect any discrete changes in rates to be smaller than under the present system. And there is a reasonable hope that under the gliding parity the average divergence from the equilibrium exchange rates over time would be less than under the present movable peg. Whether or not, on balance, disequilibrating capital flows would be greater or less than under the present system therefore, I find it very difficult to say.

Refusal to Glide

I carry the argument one stage further. It would be my feeling that governments, fearing precisely the effect on speculation that I have described, fearing in other words that if they allow a small change it will be taken as evidence of their view as to the necessity for a larger one, will exercise their discretion by refusing to glide, thus frustrating the whole system. Now the counter argument generally put forward, the one which Dick also mentioned, namely, that any effect that the glide may have on capital flows can be offset by an appropriate interest rate policy, seems to me to be decidedly oversimplified. It is not so easy, I would submit, to gauge the interest difference that would be required to offset any given speculative capital flow. Nor would it be easy to gauge the additional interest difference required to offset the effects on exchange in anticipation of a decision to crawl at a given rate for a longer period of time. Countries in deficit usually have high interest rates anyhow, and it may be politically difficult to raise them further. If, as I have argued, resort to the glide intensified the capital flow, monetary policy, as we all well know, cannot be so easily pre-empted to meet needs of the balance of payments, if only because fiscal policies are not sufficiently under government control that one can rely on them to offset the domestic effects of the changes in monetary policy which are adopted for balance-of-payments reasons.

I have been speaking, of course, about the effects of the gliding parity in its discretionary form. I have said the Cooper form of the gliding parity is not the pure discretionary system. Countries unable to justify to other trading nations their persistent refusal to glide, when reserve movements indicate that they should, would in his scheme expose themselves to international sanctions. But if a country were to state its considered judgment that it could make a required exchange rate adjustment with less disturbance by discrete jumps than by a glide, I seriously doubt whether any international body would presume to override it, much less to apply sanctions. At the most it might use admonitions or recommendations. To find a middle way between automatism and discretion is something that appeals to the compromiser in all of us, but it is as difficult as it is desirable. I fear that the Cooper compromise would in practice end up closer to the discretionary end than to the automatic end of the spectrum of possibilities. If I am right, that the gliding peg to the extent that it is used, to the extent that the authorities allow it to be used, is as likely to intensify as to mitigate payments disequilibria, then it would be rash to expect from it any great improvements as far as abstention from payments restrictions is concerned. By the same token, however, I would not expect this to have the relaxing effect on monetary discipline that some people are afraid of.

Personally, I think exchange rate flexibility will in the end have to be sought in a much more market-determined system than the international financial community is as yet willing to contemplate. And the best to be hoped for in the present juncture is increased tolerance of experimentation in this direction by developed countries as well as underdeveloped countries on an individual basis. However, I don't want to end my comments on Cooper's version of the gliding parity on too negative a note. If his presumptive rules are followed, and if sufficient international liquidity were made available to counteract the increase in speculation that I would anticipate from the crawling peg in its discretionary form, then I would agree that it might be possible to neutralize the disadvantages of the scheme while retaining its advantages. These advantages, to repeat, are that countries should be able most of the time to keep their exchange rates closer to their long-term equilibrium level, and should also be able to adjust their economies more smoothly to changes in that level than under the present system.

The Costs of Adjustment via Controls and an Alternative

NORMAN S. FIELEKE

Balance-of-payments controls are sometimes referred to as devices for avoiding balance-of-payments adjustment. Whatever is meant by this reference, the fact is, of course, that controls can eliminate an imbalance in international payments, but at a cost that is not commonly associated with nonselective or market mechanisms. The balance-of-payments gains and the welfare costs resulting from the controls now employed in this country are subjects which merit investigation, in view of the reliance placed upon these controls as a tool of balance-of-payments policy in recent years. In particular, if the ratio of balance-of-payments gain to welfare cost is not the same at the margin for all the controls, there is a *prima facie* case for adjusting the controls so as to make the ratio the same. More fundamentally, if the welfare costs associated with the controls are significant in relation to the balance-of-payments gains, there is reason to explore the feasibility of alternative balance-of-payments adjustment techniques which presumably are free of such costs.

As a first step in examining these questions, this paper investigates the balance-of-payments and welfare effects of two familiar controls: the "Buy-American" policy and the tying of foreign aid. The second part considers a possible alternative to such controls.

The Defense Department's Buy-American Policy

Under the Buy-American policy, the United States Government grants price preferences to domestic goods in deciding whether to purchase domestic or competing foreign goods. Roughly speaking, the Department of Defense purchases domestic goods unless their price is more than 50 percent above the cost of comparable foreign goods. Other Federal agencies also grant a 50 percent price preference to domestic goods if the goods purchased are to be used abroad, but the preference is usually only 6 percent if the goods are to be used in this country.

The 50 percent preferences were instituted in order to reduce the

Mr. Fieleke is Assistant Vice President and Senior Economist, Federal Reserve Bank of Boston, Boston, Massachusetts.

balance-of-payments deficit, and I have estimated both the balance-of-payments effect and the welfare cost of the preference as employed by the Department of Defense, which accounts for the great bulk of Federal procurement of foreign commodities. The derivation of these estimates has been published elsewhere;[1] at this point I shall merely report my finding that, during the years 1963 and 1964, the Defense Department's practices reduced the deficit by roughly $26 million per year, at a welfare cost of roughly $14 million per year.[2]

This welfare cost was estimated with techniques appropriate for estimating the welfare losses from tariffs.[3] It is welfare cost to the world, not to this country, although there are some grounds for thinking that this country bears most of it. While it would be interesting to know the welfare effect on this country, the estimation of this effect would be very difficult, if not impossible, with the data at hand.[4] Moreover, the welfare cost to the world may be the more relevant measure. The United States has erected its controls without specific retaliation by other nations, so that the rest of the world can be said, in a sense, to have sanctioned the use of controls by this country as a means of balance-of-payments adjustment. Under this view, the welfare cost is the cost to the world of reducing the U.S. deficit by means of the controls adopted.

---

[1] Norman S. Fieleke, "The Buy-American Policy of the United States Government: its balance-of-payments and welfare effects," *New England Economic Review* (Boston: Federal Reserve Bank of Boston), July/August, 1969.

[2] These estimates do not include the effects of any preferences accorded domestic goods under the Military Assistance Program, nonappropriated fund purchases, and purchases of petroleum.

[3] For such estimates by others, see Harry G. Johnson, "The Gains from Freer Trade with Europe: An Estimate," *The Manchester School of Economic and Social Studies*, XXVI (September, 1958), 247-55; Tibor Scitovsky, *Economic Theory and Western European Integration* (Stanford: Stanford University Press, 1958), pp. 52-70; Arnold C. Harberger, "Using the Resources at Hand More Effectively," *The American Economic Review, Papers and Proceedings*, XLIX (May, 1959), 134-46; J. Wemelsfelder, "The Short-Term Effect of the Lowering of Import Duties in Germany," *The Economic Journal*, LXX (March, 1960), 94-104; Robert M. Stern, "The U.S. Tariff and the Efficiency of the U.S. Economy," *The American Economic Review, Papers and Proceedings*, LIV (May, 1964), 459-70; and Giorgio M. Basevi, "The Restrictive Effect of the U.S. Tariff and Its Welfare Value," *The American Economic Review*, LVIII (September, 1968), 840-52.

[4] For an idea of the difficulties in appraising the effects of controls on national welfare, see Ronald W. Jones, "International Capital Movements and the Theory of Tariffs and Trade," *The Quarterly Journal of Economics*, LXXXI (February, 1967), 1-38.

Aid-tying by AID

The tying of foreign aid also has its costs. "Tying," of course, simply means requiring that U.S. aid be spent in some sense on U.S. goods and services; it can be viewed as an attempted compulsory transfer mechanism. Since 1959, when tying was begun, its main target has been the programs now administered by the Agency for International Development (AID). Before 1959, the commodities purchased under these programs were generally obtained in the cheapest Free-World market. Then in October, 1959, commodity procurement from development loan funds was generally limited to U.S. goods, and in December, 1960, procurement from grant money was generally prohibited in 19 advanced countries. Thereafter, the trend toward more complete tying continued, and in January, 1968, the Treasury Department reported that, "The only significant elements in the A.I.D. program not specifically tied to U.S. goods and services are salaries and payments to A.I.D. overseas personnel and contractors . . . and limited offshore procurement for A.I.D. administrative purposes."[5] In addition, U.S. flag vessels must be used to transport at least half of the gross tonnage of all commodities which are financed with AID dollar funds and are transported to the recipient country on ocean vessels.

There have been some second-thoughts about tying, and a few months ago certain tying measures designed to ensure "additionality" were discontinued. The purpose of these additionality measures was to ensure that AID-financed exports would add to, rather than replace, other U.S. exports. Even though they have been discontinued, these measures merit discussion, for at least two reasons.[6] First, they nicely illustrate the contradictions which can beset balance-of-payments controls. Second, and more to the point of this paper, most of these measures, like other aid-tying measures, were not well designed to reduce the U.S. deficit.

For example, under the additionality program AID refused to finance the export of goods of which the United States was a net importer, apparently on the assumption that such goods when shipped from the United States would be replaced by imports. On

[5] U.S., Department of the Treasury, *Maintaining the Strength of the United States Dollar in a Strong Free World Economy* (Washington, D.C.: U.S. Government Printing Office, January, 1968), Tab C, p. 1. In this paper AID's contributions to international organizations are ignored.

[6] For a description of these measures, see U.S., Department of the Treasury, *op. cit.*, Tab C, pp. 4-7.

the other hand, later guidelines forbade procurement of goods in which the United States had a price advantage or was strongly competitive in foreign markets; the reasoning was that other countries would buy these goods from the United States even without assistance from AID. Now, if AID did not finance goods of which the United States was a net importer and did not finance goods in which the United States competed vigorously in foreign markets, the agency had little choice but to finance those goods and services which were not very likely to be traded internationally on a commercial basis. But the typical nontraded items, such as shoeshines and highways, offer certain transportation problems!

In practice, the agency no doubt found room within its guidelines to finance the export of items in which the United States had a relatively weak export position. But, again, the underlying logic is not clear. If AID is to select goods for financing so as to improve the U.S. balance of trade in the short run, static theory suggests that the goods financed should be those for which there is a high degree of elasticity in the U.S. export supply schedule, in the aggregate export supply of U.S. competitors, and in the import demand of the aided country. It would be pure coincidence if such goods were selected under the agency's standards either now or during the experiment with "additionality."[7]

The case for selecting goods with the elasticities just recommended is based upon the assumption that AID financing could be designed to effect a downward shift in the supply schedule of a selected U.S. export to an aided country. Such a shift would result in a relatively large increase in U.S. export proceeds if there were substantial elasticity in the import demand in the aided country, in the U.S. export supply, and in the export supply by U.S. competitors. In addition, complementarity between the demand for the subsidized exports and other U.S. exports would be desirable, as it would enhance the immediate export gain from subsidization, while a relationship of substitutability would diminish the gain.

The question, then, is how AID financing could be tailored to shift downward the supply schedules of such U.S. exports to a less-developed country. The techniques presently employed by AID

---

[7]That the agency's efforts to ensure additionality met with little success was recently confirmed by Administrator William S. Gaud: "... all of our additionality efforts have saved us about $35 million a year over the last 4 years, which isn't much." See U.S., Congress, Subcommittee of the Joint Economic Committee, *Hearings, A Review of Balance of Payments Policies*, 91st Cong., 1st sess., 1969, p. 88.

probably do not achieve this end. In essence, they present the less-developed country with a grant or low-interest loan, which the country must then match with the importation of approved U.S. commodities, but they provide no price incentive for the country to increase its purchases of those commodities above the "normal" level. Thus, doubt arises whether the country is using AID financing to purchase an amount of a commodity which would have been purchased in any case.

In theory, one way of dealing with the problem would be to make AID assistance available in the form of subsidies on designated U.S. exports to aided countries. This technique seems preferable to requesting less-developed countries to use exchange controls to attain a specified level of imports from the United States, although the controls now employed in those countries might have to be modified so as to permit the U.S. export subsidies to have an appreciable effect.

The intent of the foregoing analysis is not to aid and abet the conversion of AID into an export-promotion agency, but to indicate that if immediate export expansion is in fact an overriding goal, there may be more effective means of pursuing it than the tying measures that have been employed.

But the welfare effects of aid-tying have been even less laudable. In this connection, the efforts to attain additionality bring sharply into focus the dilemma which is posed by all the customary forms of tying. If tying is to increase U.S. exports, it must force aid recipients to purchase U.S. goods which they would not buy on the basis of commercial considerations, goods which they could purchase more cheaply from sources other than this country. Consequently, when tying succeeds in improving our balance of payments, it also reduces the real value of our aid to the recipients. Not long ago AID Administrator William S. Gaud reported that the U.S. goods sold to less-developed countries under the additionality program sometimes cost those countries 40 percent more than comparable non-U.S. goods.[8]

On the other hand, it is sometimes argued that a substantially smaller volume of funds would be allocated for foreign aid if tying were discontinued, on the grounds that the majority of the Congress and the public wish to see the money spent on U.S. goods, particularly while the U.S. balance of payments is in deficit. Yet the

[8] *Ibid.*, pp. 88-89.

fact that we have given less aid than the nominal amount may be one of the reasons that our aid programs are so frequently criticized for failing to progress toward their objectives, a criticism which in turn provides a basis for less ample funding.

What is the balance-of-payments gain and welfare cost associated with aid-tying? Using the same techniques that were employed in the case of the Buy-American policy, I estimate that the tying of aid by AID resulted in a welfare cost of some $29 million in 1963, in exchange for a reduction of roughly $86 million in the U.S. balance-of-payments deficit.

Cost and Effectiveness

Neither these estimates nor those quoted for Buy-American should be regarded as precise; they are merely rough orders of magnitude. Even allowing for a wide margin of error, however, the reductions in the deficit resulting from Buy-American and aid-tying are strikingly small, at least during the periods examined. One reason is that the feedback effects appear to be fairly high; to illustrate, a controlled reduction of $1 in U.S. imports typically diminishes foreign purchases of U.S. exports by something on the order of $0.60, according to a recent analysis by Piekarz and Stekler.[9]

It is interesting to compute the ratio of balance-of-payments gain to welfare cost for each of these two controls. For the Defense Department's Buy-American policy, the ratio of balance-of-payments gain to welfare cost is not quite 2, while for the tying of aid by AID, the ratio is about 3. Given the fact that these two controls were in use in 1963, should not these ratios have been equal?[10] Should not the tying of aid have been more intensive, and the Buy-American policy less intensive, in order to achieve the same total reduction in the balance-of-payments deficit at a lower welfare cost?

The answer to this question requires a value judgment regarding

[9] Rolf Piekarz and Lois Ernstoff Stekler, "Induced Changes in Trade and Payments," *The Review of Economics and Statistics*, XLIX (November, 1967), 522-24.

[10] Strictly speaking, it is ratios of marginal rather than total quantities that are pertinent. However, the derivation of the marginal quantities would require more data than has been available to us, and an argument from equal ignorance might justify the use of the totals. For an indication of data required to ascertain the marginal magnitudes, see J. E. Meade, *The Theory of International Economic Policy*, Vol. II: *Trade and Welfare* (New York: Oxford University Press, 1955), pp. 554-55.

the welfare costs of each control.[11] The welfare cost estimates presented in this paper are "neutral" in the sense that they assume a dollar yields the same satisfaction to everybody, and the estimates should therefore be adjusted in accordance with one's opinion concerning the worth of an extra dollar to those most directly affected by the controls. To venture my own opinion, no further research is needed to show that much higher welfare weights should attach to the dollars in which the welfare costs of aid-tying are measured than to the dollars in which the costs of Buy-American are measured.

Is There Really a Deficit to Be Controlled?

Are there less costly means of dealing with the balance-of-payments deficit? There are at least two lines of reasoning which suggest an affirmative answer. The first denies that the United States has in fact had a deficit in the customary sense. Perhaps the most persuasive argument in support of this view attributes the U.S. "deficit" to the demand of other countries for reserves in excess of the supply from non-U.S. sources.[12] If this argument is correct, there is little point in imposing controls or, indeed, in taking the other customary measures designed merely to eliminate the deficit, for such measures would either fail or impose their own welfare burdens.

In my view, there is some basis for believing that part of the U.S. deficit has indeed resulted from the demand of other countries for international reserve assets.[13] To be sure, a potentially superior source of reserve growth, the creation of special drawing rights, is now on the threshold; but insofar as *past* U.S. deficits have reflected the reserve demands of other countries, there has been little point to the use of controls or of other customary balance-of-payments adjustment techniques.

However, it remains to be shown that *all* of the deficit, or even most of it, has been merely the reflection of a demand for reserves.

[11] Such judgments cannot be avoided "if welfare analysis in international trade is to be more than a curiosity or a self-denying ordinance." See Richard E. Caves, *Trade and Economic Structure: Models and Methods* (Cambridge, Mass.: Harvard University Press, 1960), p. 232.

[12] For example, see Robert A. Mundell, "Real Gold, Dollars, and Paper Gold," *The American Economic Review, Papers and Proceedings*, LIX (May, 1969), 324-31.

[13] For example, see Piekarz and Stekler, *op. cit.*, 525-26.

Given the degree of inflation in the world in recent years, one suspects that the reserves held outside of this country have not been so inadequate as to justify such a strong conclusion.[14]

The Movable Band

But there is a second and perhaps more convincing line of reasoning to suggest that we need not carry the welfare burdens imposed by the controls. The point is that there appear to be other means of reducing imbalances in international payments which do not entail such losses. My own preference runs to a modest widening of the range about parity within which a rate of exchange is now permitted to fluctuate, together with more frequent and smaller adjustments of the parity itself. The parity on a given day might be set equal to a moving average of the market rates observed over a preceding period, so that governments would be spared the traumatic experience of having to decide when and how much to change the parity.[15] The case for such a movable band has been ably presented by others,[16] and I wish merely to venture a few opinions on some particular details of design and negotiating strategy. Of course, I appreciate that some countries might be well advised to peg their currencies to the currencies of other countries.

The Degree of Exchange-Rate Flexibility

A fundamental problem regarding the design of the movable band is the degree of flexibility it should provide. In other words, how

[14]Cf. Gottfried Haberler, *Money in the International Economy* (Cambridge, Mass.: Harvard University Press, 1965), pp. 45-46.

[15]Some "non-market" transactions between governments do not influence market exchange rates directly, but it does not necessarily follow that observed market rates would constitute a poor guide over the long run to what exchange rates should be. Market rates are surely influenced indirectly, if not directly, by intergovernmental transactions, for speculators are far from oblivious to the impact of such transactions on governmental reserve positions. But if "non-market" transactions did not affect market rates, it would not be obvious why we should be greatly concerned about them from the standpoint of balance-of-payments policy. If they don't matter, they don't matter.

[16]The writer's thinking was strongly influenced by J. Black's article, "A Proposal for the Reform of Exchange Rates," *Economic Journal*, LXXVI (June, 1966), 288-95. A bibliography on the subject of greater (but limited) exchange-rate flexibility should also include the following works: William Fellner, "On Limited Exchange-Rate Flexibility" in William Fellner, *et al.*, *Maintaining and Restoring Balance in International Payments* (Princeton: Princeton University Press, 1966), pp. 111-22; George N. Halm, *The Band Proposal: The Limits of Permissible Exchange Rate Variations* (Princeton: Princeton University, 1965);

wide should the band be, and how rapidly should it be allowed to move? While precise answers to these questions are probably beyond the ken of mortal man, at least at this stage of the art, it may not be difficult to specify the most relevant considerations. These considerations seem to call for a very limited degree of flexibility.

One consideration which favors a small, rather than a large, amount of flexibility is uncertainty over the role which speculation would play if flexibility were great. There is considerable disagreement on this matter, but on the basis of arguments advanced by Viner, Meade, and others, the possibility that destabilizing speculation could arise under a highly flexible system seems real enough to warrant a less revolutionary change.[17] More flexibility could be introduced at a later date if experience seemed to warrant it.

A second argument for only a modest degree of flexibility is that, for better or worse, institutions have grown up and investments have been made under the regime of fixed exchange rates; and even if a high degree of flexibility were desired as a long-run goal, it might be a bit harsh to cast all past commitments adrift suddenly on the seas of greatly expanded flexibility. In particular, a little time might be required for the development of economical hedging facilities. That far-reaching social changes should sometimes be introduced gradually, so as to reduce the harm experienced by those injured, is not a new idea in the field of political economy. The Kennedy Round tariff reductions, for example, were staged over a period of five years.

Finally, the degree of flexibility built into the system should be small enough that governments, applying whatever criteria they deem relevant, would pledge to allow that flexibility full rein. Provision

George N. Halm, *Toward Limited Exchange-Rate Flexibility* (Princeton: Princeton University, 1969); Douglas Jay, "Time for the Crawling Peg," *International Currency Review*, June, 1969, pp. 5-11; George W. McKenzie, "International Monetary Reform and the 'Crawling Peg,' " *Federal Reserve Bank of St. Louis Review*, 51 (February, 1969), 15-23, and also the *Comment* and *Reply* in the same *Review*, 51 (July, 1969), 21-31; J. E. Meade, "The International Monetary Mechanism," *The Three Banks Review*, September, 1964, pp. 3-25; J. E. Meade, "Exchange Rate Flexibility," *The Three Banks Review*, June, 1966, pp. 3-27; J. Carter Murphy, "Moderated Exchange Rate Variability," *The National Banking Review*, 3 (December, 1965), 151-61, and also the *Comment* and *Reply* in the same *Review*, 4 (September, 1966), 97-105; John H. Williamson, *The Crawling Peg* (Princeton: Princeton University, 1965); and Leland B. Yeager, "A Skeptical View of the 'Band' Proposal," *The National Banking Review*, 4 (March, 1967), 291-97, and also the *Comments* and *Reply* in the same *Review*, 4 (June, 1967), 511-18.

[17]See Jacob Viner, "Some International Aspects of Economic Stabilization" in L. D. White, ed., *The State of the Social Sciences* (Chicago: University of Chicago Press, 1955), pp. 283-98; and J. E. Meade, "Exchange-Rate Flexibility," *The Three Banks Review*, June, 1966, pp. 14-15.

should be made to apply sanctions, such as discriminatory trade restrictions, against nations which violated this pledge. The alternative to such a procedure might well be conflicting interventions by governments in the foreign exchange market and exchange rates that were even less realistic than some of those observed in recent years. Of course, there would be no limitations on governmental efforts to influence exchange rates through aggregative fiscal and monetary policies. Even so, the objection is sometimes raised that governments simply will not refrain from direct intervention in the foreign exchange market, even within a fairly narrow band. This issue can only be settled by governments, but the economist can at least point out that any scheme for increased exchange-rate flexibility to adjust balances of payments ultimately requires governments to reduce the extent of their direct intervention in the foreign exchange market. If this requirement for less intervention were clearly recognized in the design of the scheme, as proposed here, there would probably be fewer misunderstandings and less need for arm-twisting negotiations once the scheme had been put into effect.

The foregoing considerations suggest that the degree of flexibility should be small, and, indeed, very little flexibility would be required to adjust balances of payments during periods of tranquility; but quite a bit could be required during storms of social protest. In fact, in times of great crisis little short of unlimited flexibility would suffice if rapid adjustments were to be made in balances of payments. But it is precisely in these times that destabilizing speculation is most likely to appear, so that great flexibility would not be so appropriate in these periods as slower changes in exchange rates enforced by the use of international reserves, international lending, and controls as a last resort.

The conclusion, then, is that the extent of flexibility in exchange rates should be small. Exactly how wide the band should be, and exactly how fast it should be permitted to move, are questions for negotiation and for further research.

One approach to these questions would be to identify each imbalance which has resulted in an abrupt parity change or in the imposition of significant controls in recent years and then to estimate the degree of flexibility which would have substituted for the abrupt parity change or the controls. In this way, some idea could be obtained of the maximum degree of flexibility which would be required during relatively normal periods. If this degree of flexibility did not exceed that which governments considered wise, bearing in mind the arguments for very limited flexibility, there would be no problem. But if it did exceed what governments considered wise, the supply of reserves and emergency lending would have to be adequate to allow deficit countries time to adjust by means of the limited flexibility and other measures available to them.

A Difficulty with Gradual Parity Adjustments

There is, however, a fundamental objection to gradual adjustments of parities. Should it become a "sure thing" that a country's currency will undergo the maximum permissible depreciation over the course of an ensuing time period, the country might experience a massive capital outflow unless its interest rates were kept sufficiently above interest rates abroad to offset the lure of currency appreciation abroad. But if a country's interest rate policy is to be dictated by balance-of-payments considerations, one of the main pillars supporting the case for gradual parity adjustments is substantially weakened, if not shattered.[18]

There might be little difficulty if short-term interest rates alone could be adapted to balance-of-payments requirements, leaving long-term rates and fiscal policy to maintain internal balance. However, the idea that monetary and fiscal magnitudes can be tailored that carefully in today's world should appear extremely naive to those who have observed the difficulties confronting economic management in recent years. In this country, for example, not only can there be stalemates between the legislative and executive branches, so that fiscal magnitudes run substantially out of control, but the accuracy with which we can predict the influence of changes in fiscal and monetary policy leaves much to be desired.

But perhaps the proposal for gradual changes in parities can still be rescued. Suppose there were no reason to doubt that a currency would depreciate by the maximum permissible amount, say, 2 percent, in terms of its parity over the coming year.[19] To forestall a disruptive capital outflow the government could then impose an interest equalization tax of 2 percent on the capital outflows most affected by the impending depreciation and an interest equalization subsidy of 2 percent on the capital inflows most affected, maintain-

[18]That pillar, of course, is the argument that monetary policy would be more available for the pursuit of domestic goals.

[19]The French franc after the social disturbances of May, 1968, would have been such a currency, had a system of gradual parity changes then been in operation.

ing this tax and subsidy only so long as the continued depreciation of its currency was commonly expected, *and only so long as the approval of the International Monetary Fund was forthcoming.* Unlike the present controls, these would impose no welfare losses, if properly administered. Of course, questions would arise as to which capital flows should be taxed and subsidized, and leakages would undoubtedly develop. The goal, however, is not impeccability, merely workability — and that could perhaps be attained.

Another suggestion for coping with this problem of disruptive capital movements is to allow only minuscule changes in parities each year. Unfortunately, this proposal virtually abandons the very flexibility which made a change seem attractive in the first place. However, if a workable system of interest-equalization taxes and subsidies could not be designed, minuscule short-run changes in parities would be preferable to no short-run changes, although under such a system large, abrupt parity changes of the sort that now cause so much grief would occasionally be required.

Some Negotiating Considerations

Suppose that one of the plans for increased flexibility were to receive the endorsement of the Government of the United States. How could other governments be persuaded of its desirability? What should be the balance-of-payments strategy of this country?

At the risk of venturing too deeply into unknown political territory, I would urge that careful consideration be given to the following approach. First, we should announce that our balance-of-payments controls will be removed in stages over the course of the next two years. Second, we should inform other governments that it would be difficult for us to convert any of their dollar holdings into gold at the rate of $35 an ounce until currency exchange rates have been made somewhat more flexible so as to provide us with an alternative to unemployment for adjusting our balance of payments in the short run.

If other countries were to oppose the introduction of a *little* more flexibility, one of their alternatives would be to advocate a *lot* more flexibility, that is, a freely floating dollar; and it is not clear why they would choose this alternative over limited flexibility, given their apparent preference for the present system of virtually *no* (short-run) flexibility. But if the dollar were allowed to float freely, the consequences for the United States would probably be no worse than under the present system, even if destabilizing speculation did occasionally arise, because trade with foreign countries is a relatively small magnitude in the U.S. economy. The other option facing other countries would be to peg their currencies to the dollar, and the consequences of such pegging probably need not concern us, for reasons that have been stated elsewhere by Milton Friedman.[20]

Implications for International Trade

In conclusion, I should like to offer an observation on what is probably the most common objection to the proposal for greater exchange-rate flexibility. The objection is that greater flexibility would substantially reduce international trade by introducing more risk into international transactions. Of course, it is seldom if ever explained why efficient hedging facilities would fail to develop in accordance with the demand for them, and it is seldom mentioned that controls, the adopted alternative to flexibility, substantially impede trade themselves.

In this connection, the Research and Policy Committee of the Committee for Economic Development has just made an interesting proposal for balance-of-payments adjustment. The Committee suggests that border taxes on imports and rebates on exports be varied temporarily in order to help correct imbalances in international payments; the Committee prefers such variations to quotas as a balance-of-payments measure.[21] Since such variations in border taxes and export rebates are equivalent to variations in exchange rates on current account, it appears that the business community may not be so fearful of a little more flexibility as some have believed, particularly if the alternative is controls.

---

[20]Milton Friedman in "Round Table on Exchange Rate Policy," *The American Economic Review, Papers and Proceedings,* LIX (May, 1969), 365.

[21]*Nontariff Distortions of Trade* (New York: Committee for Economic Development, 1969), 22-23.

DISCUSSION

RALPH C. BRYANT

It was said of Disraeli that his idea of an agreeable man was someone who agreed with him. Following that maxim, I find Norm Fieleke a very agreeable person. By and large, I am in substantial agreement with what I take to be the main propositions of his paper: namely, that selective restrictions over international transactions can be, in almost all circumstances, a very costly balance-of-payments adjustment device; and that the direction in which one should look for alternative devices should be towards changes in exchange rates. There are several minor things in Norm's paper with which I disagree, and, like all discussants, I will emphasize areas of disagreement and differences in nuance. However, I do not want my discussion of these differences to camouflage the fact that I am in broad agreement with his main propositions.

The Costs of Selective Controls

Perhaps the most interesting part of Norm's paper is the section in which he tries to estimate the static welfare costs and the balance-of-payments gains resulting from the Buy-American policy and the policy of tying aid. In the paper he read to you, he did not fully spell out the procedures he used to derive these estimates. There are 10 sweeping generalizations for every empirically-supported fact in international finance, and much more analysis of the type carried out by Fieleke needs to be done.

I do not think I would want to put much weight on the specific estimates that Norm has derived. He, himself, is well aware that there is a big variance around such estimates. For example, his calculations make use of some elasticities of demand and supply that were generated in a study by Floyd; I suspect that these elasticities are a bit on the high side — at the least, they are certainly (as Floyd intended them to be) very *long-run* elasticities. I think one can also quarrel with the estimates of reflection ratios in the Piekarz-Stekler study that Fieleke employs in deriving his estimated costs and benefits.

It would be helpful, I think, to give you an idea of how sensitive Fieleke's calculations are to changes in some of these assumptions.

Mr. Bryant is Assistant to the Director, Division of International Finance, Board of Governors of the Federal Reserve System, Washington, D.C.

Just to illustrate, consider the estimate of the reflection ratio for the United States — that is to say, the amount by which U.S. exports will be reduced if the United States buys $1 less from foreign countries, after feedbacks and interdependences have worked their way through the system. Piekarz and Stekler in their study come up with an average ratio of about 60 cents — and this is the estimate that Norm uses. This seems to me quite high, especially if we are thinking about U.S. military procurement in Europe. Most of these countries, if we judge on an *a priori* basis, are not that sensitive to changes in their export earnings. For the sake of illustration, I have assumed that the right number may be closer to 30 cents. I would guess that $.30 is too low; $.60 seems clearly too high; the correct figure probably lies somewhere in between. If we were to assume a value of the reflection ratio of $.30, we would roughly double the balance-of-payments gain that Norm has estimated. For example, instead of having an improvement in the balance of payments of $86 million from tying aid, we might get a number like $170 million. Similarly, the welfare cost, instead of being something like $29 or $30 million, would be more like $55 or $60 million.

Time Pattern of Costs and Benefits

In calculating the static welfare costs and the balance-of-payments gains resulting from imposition of selective restrictions on international transactions, the time pattern of the costs and benefits is not irrelevant. It is certainly true over time that costs cumulate and feedback effects reduce the initial gross balance-of-payments gains. However, there are reasons to think that the gross balance-of-payments gains occur in the short run and that it is only after perhaps as much as three or four years that the full costs and offsets are realized. If there were anything to the rationalization used by the U.S. Government when these restrictions were first imposed — namely that they were merely temporary and that fundamental adjustment in our balance of payments was genuinely taking place — then I suppose the arguments in favor of imposing these controls become marginally more acceptable than if one takes Fieleke's estimates at face value. I don't want to give too much weight to this point, however, because as we all know, controls imposed for temporary reasons often, perhaps nearly always, turn out not to be so temporary after all.

I think it is also useful to remind you more specifically than Norm has done of the other costs associated with selective restrictions. These are not quantifiable, but I think I would give at least as much weight to these non-quantifiable costs as I do to the static welfare costs that Norm has estimated. The kind of thing I have in mind is the smaller exposure to international competition which U.S. firms face which may, in the long run, result in slower adoption of new technology and slower growth; administrative costs such as those of the capital control programs which have often necessitated substantial reorganization of the financial structures and methods of operations of corporations; the opportunity cost of the substantial amounts of legal, accounting, and other management resources that have to be devoted to preparing reports, filing requests, and interpreting complex regulations; and so on. In Washington, when the mandatory Commerce control program came out, it was widely referred to as a relief bill for the legal profession.

Despite a passing comment in Norm's paper that other countries have allowed the United States to impose selective controls and thus, in some sense, have actually accepted them, and that therefore the appropriate welfare cost to measure is the cost of the U.S. controls to the world as a whole, I myself think that a "demonstration effect" is also quite important and needs to be taken into account. If the United States resorts to fairly extensive use of selective controls — as we have — and especially if foreign countries emulate the United States — as I think to some extent they have, either because they are worried about the impacts on their own economies and retaliate for that reason, or simply because they further succumb to protectionist pressures in their economies and use the U.S. actions as an excuse — the costs to all countries of using selective restrictions as a balance-of-payments adjustment device can cumulate quickly. It just cannot be helpful to have the major trading country in the system leading the way on this front. Chaucer wrote about the good parson: "If gold ruste, what will iron do?" Perhaps that metallic reference isn't quite appropriate in this gathering. Nonetheless, it is very clear that if the town mayor goes around picking flowers in the public park, it can't help but induce some of the other citizens to throw off their inhibitions, too.

The major thing I find missing from the first section of Fieleke's paper is an attempt to place his estimates of the balance-of-payments gains and static welfare costs more into perspective with the costs and benefits associated with the other broad policy possibilities. In particular, Norm refers to "nonselective" or market mechanisms as not having the costs associated with selective controls, but does not specifically note that one of the main alternative policies — the use of (nonselective) fiscal and monetary policies — can have very high costs indeed.

If the level of demand in an economy is inappropriate on domestic grounds alone, then obviously the situation needs to be rectified with fiscal and monetary policies in any case. If demand-management measures would help improve the balance of payments, that is only another good reason to get the level of demand right. Indeed, if a country is in balance-of-payments difficulties and lets its exchange rate adjust *without* also attempting to achieve an appropriate level and rate of growth of demand, it will invariably still find itself in hot water.

Cost of Adjusting the Balance of Payments
by Demand Management

If the level and rate of growth of domestic demand are already roughly appropriate, however, then the costs of adjusting the balance-of-payments via demand management can be much greater than the costs of adjusting via selective controls. This proposition is generally true, but *a fortiori* true of the United States. Suppose we take a number like $200-300 million as the net balance-of-payments effect of completely removing all the AID procedures for tying aid. Even AID itself would only come up with an estimate on the order of $½ billion, so $200-300 million is probably a reasonable number. (It is significantly higher than the estimate in Norm's paper, but substantially lower than official estimates.) What costs would be incurred in obtaining the same $200-300 million balance-of-payments improvement by deflating aggregate demand, assuming we started from a situation in which demand and employment were growing along benchmark "high-employment" paths chosen by policy makers?

In order to get a *net* improvement of $200-300 million in the balance of payments by lowering domestic demand, U.S. imports would have to be reduced by a multiple of that amount — perhaps by $500 million or more, if one uses an estimate of the reflection ratio as high as the one employed by Piekarz-Stekler and Fieleke. (I am ignoring capital movements in these crude calculations, as Fieleke does and virtually everyone else who attempts quantitative estimates.) The average propensity to import in the United States is now perhaps 6 per cent. Suppose one assumes a very high number for the marginal propensity to import, say as high as 20 per cent. That surely is on the high side for periods without excess demand; it has been that high recently, but would not be if the United States economy were successfully moving along a "high-employment" growth path. Regardless of the specific value one picks for the marginal propensity to import, it is quite clear that to get a $500 million reduction in imports — which would yield a net gain of $200 million or $300 million in the balance of payments — would require at least a $2½-$3 billion reduction in GNP below the "high-employment" level. The calculation can even be taken further if one is willing to employ a crude rule like Okun's Law. Roughly speaking, a reduction of $2½ billion in GNP might increase unemployment from 4 percent — if that were the target unemployment rate along the growth path — to perhaps 4.1 percent, or possibly as much as 4.2 percent.

However one does the calculations, it is obvious that an output loss measured in the billions will completely overshadow anything like the $100-$200 million costs associated by Fieleke with tied-aid. Thus if it were the case that the United States were forced to choose only between demand management and selective controls as balance-of-payments adjustment policies, there would be absolutely no question about which to choose in a noninflationary demand situation. One does not use an elephant gun to shoot woodchucks; it is not advisable to crack nuts with a steamhammer; demand-management policies should not be used in the United States to deal with balance-of-payments difficulties when the evolution of domestic demand is already judged to be appropriate.

Perhaps I am, as in the old Russian proverb, beating down an open door and doing it very vigorously. I doubt that Fieleke would disagree with this last proposition. Nevertheless, his paper does suffer from shifting rather quickly to a discussion in Part II of exchange-rate changes after a discussion in the first section of the costs of adjustment by controls. These latter costs can only be evaluated in relation to the costs associated with alternative feasible policies. Compared with at least some of the alternative feasible policies, the costs of selective controls must be judged to be fairly small beans.

U.S. Policy in the 1960's in Retrospect

What might a balanced verdict be of U.S. policy in the last decade? I am sure I cannot be completely objective, but I will briefly sketch out here the way in which I would draw up the balance sheet.

There are four broad possibilities of dealing with a payments imbalance: (1) selective restrictions (2) the general use of fiscal and monetary measures (3) achieving changes in exchange rates, or (4) simply financing the imbalance rather than trying to eliminate it. It is very clear that what the United States actually did in the 1960's was to finance — that is probably the most important policy we followed — and then secondly, we imposed various selective controls. The second possibility, at least the deflation of aggregate demand substantially below the level that would have been appropriate on domestic grounds, was correctly ruled out because of the very high costs.

The real question is: was the United States negligent in not making much greater use of exchange rates? That is an extremely complicated question, as has been noted several times already in this conference. My own opinion — which I won't try to defend here — is that a discrete change in the par value of the United States would have been a short-sighted, mistaken policy. It may not have been impossible to achieve changes in relative exchange rates by that method (although I even have strong doubts on that score), but it would have had much higher costs, both political and economic, than would have made it worthwhile. If a U.S. decision to change the $35 par value is ruled out, that really leaves only two other ways of getting changes in exchange rates. Conceivably the U.S. Government could have tried the route of *force majeure*, suspending gold sales and purchases. We probably would have gotten some rate flexibility out of that policy, although it is not a sure thing how much and in what fashion. The third route would have been through multilateral negotiation of some kind of exchange-rate flexibility — perhaps one of the limited flexibility schemes that are now receiving so much attention. There are persuasive reasons for not having taken the *force majeure* route — certainly, I think, in the mid-1960's.

When I look back on policy, at least up through 1964 and 1965, therefore, it seems to me that the failure of policy was not so much the "temporary" imposition of selective restrictions. Up until that point there seemed to be reasonable grounds for hoping that price and cost trends abroad and at home were moving in directions that would eventually result in adjustment of the balance of payments without the controls, in other words, the failure of policy was not so much in imposing the restrictions, but rather in wasting the opportunity that they provided. I think we in the Government were much too slow in recognizing the need for much greater exchange-rate adjustment on a permanent and continuing basis. Even when we began to recover (I *hope* we have been recovering) from the disease of hardening of the categories, we still were very timid in taking the lead in trying to persuade other countries about the merits of greater variation in exchange rates. That of course is a very personal opinion.

After 1964 and 1965, when it became less and less plausible to believe that adjustment in the imbalance would ultimately occur if only we had enough time, and if only we pursued the right domestic stabilization policies, then it became more and more difficult —and, I think, ultimately impossible — to justify the maintenance and, *a fortiori,* the intensification of the selective restrictions.

The Alternative of Limited Flexibility

Finally, I would like to make a few random comments about the last section of Fieleke's paper where he proposes the alternative of some kind of limited flexibility scheme. A point that wasn't brought out, even in this morning's discussion and in Dick Cooper's paper, was just how severe the so-called "interest-rate constraint" would be. In Norm's view, a fundamental objection to a crawling peg scheme is that speculation would occur if the rate is depreciating (or appreciating) at the maximum permissible rate, thereby altering the effective rate of return to investors. You either, in Norm's view, have to subpoena monetary policy in order to offset these capital flows, or alternatively impose a tax and subsidy system something like the IET. My own opinion is that we have exaggerated somewhat the severity of this interest-rate constraint problem. It is true that a sudden change in expectations leading investors to anticipate, for example, a steady depreciation of the exchange rate is tantamount to an increase (though not necessarily a fully proportionate increase) in the expected rate of return earned on foreign assets. But if one analyzes the response to this change in expected rates of return in accordance with a theoretically correct model of the demand for international assets, an important component of the resulting capital flows may not be of great concern. The response would be of two sorts. One thing that will happen is that people will reallocate their existing portfolios of assets; if the expected return is higher in Country A, they will clearly hold a higher proportion of their portfolio in Country-A assets. The other thing that will happen is that there will be a change in the pattern of investment of new savings. The first of these responses, the reallocation of existing portfolios, is something that is essentially a one-shot affair. The portfolio reallocation may take quite a while to happen because of lags and so on; but, after the adjustment to the change in expected returns has occurred, there isn't any more reallocating to be done. The second type of capital movement induced by the change in expected returns, on the other hand, will go on permanently.

If one accepts this view of capital movements, and I think it is the right one, it seems clear that the capital movements that would occur in response to a change in expected returns brought about by a crawling rate would be much greater initially than they would be subsequently. That is not to say that capital movements would not be large even subsequently — the absolute magnitude of both types of flow depend on the values of the interest elasticities. But there are at least good reasons for believing that capital flows would not be as large later as they were at the beginning. As it was pointed out this morning, moreover, the incentives for capital to flow also depend on whether there is more of a "formula" variant or more of a "discretionary" variant of the crawling peg. Similarly, these incentives depend on the width of the band — the wider the band, the more uncertainty there is. Adding all these things up, I think it is quite possible that there is a little too much concern about the interest rate problem. I don't deny that it is a problem, but I wonder whether it hasn't been exaggerated.

Using Taxes to Prevent Capital Flows

What about using taxes or subsidies to "rescue" the proposal, as Fieleke suggests? I am rather doubtful. First of all, governments are not very good at knowing when markets are going to expect a change in exchange rates. We have already spoken this morning about whether markets or civil servants are better forecasters; the record of civil servants isn't very good. There are also tremendous legal and practical difficulties with applying a tax like the IET, particularly to direct investment flows. Applying such a tax without introducing serious inequities requires applying it uniformly to all capital flows. It may be possible to devise a workable uniform tax, but I am impressed by the fact that when people have looked into this question and have tried to devise such a tax, they have turned up a number of problems all of which have not by any means been solved. There is also a little bit of unconscious irony in Fieleke's proposal to use the IET in order to prevent capital flows in a limited-flexibility regime. It is a bit like the irony of using monetary policy to offset the capital flows and thereby undermining one of the pillars supporting the case for gradual parity adjustment. By the same token, it seems to me, a compensatory IET would tend to undermine another of the pillars supporting the case for gradual adjustment, namely, that exchange rates ought to be allowed to move much more flexibly so that governments will not so frequently be interfering with the free flow of goods and capital. If the government were erratically to impose and remove taxes and subsidies on capital flows, it would not make for the sort of exchange market that advocates of rate flexibiltiy usually have in mind.

Let me conclude by making a comment on the strategy which Fieleke suggests the United States should follow to get a crawling peg adopted. This strategy has two parts. The first part would be to announce that we would relax the controls, perhaps on some preannounced schedule over the next few years. The relaxation would presumably apply to all capital and current account restrictions. The second part would be to tell other countries that we would not convert dollars into gold for them until they first became "good boys" and adopted a little bit of exchange-rate flexibility.

I have some sympathy for the first part of the recommendation. At a minimum, if the balance of payments of the United States were to get worse in the next year or two — worse in the sense that it will become more clear than it has been in the last nine months that the United States does have a serious "high-employment" balance-of-payments problem — then I would certainly argue that the controls should not be intensified. On the second part of Norman's recommendation, however, I do not really see the need for telling countries that we will not convert their dollars into gold. As I said earlier, I think we want to avoid *force majeure* and perhaps even the appearance of it; substantial political costs might be incurred if the United States were to throw the gauntlet down too sharply. More-over, the choices open to other countries are not really very different, even if we tell them that the gold window at the Treasury is closed.

All we may need to do is to indicate a calm willingness to pay out gold — after next year, SDR's as well — when other countries come and ask for it. If the window has to be shut eventually, wouldn't it be better, practically and politically, for the creditors to shut it down by their own actions? The advantages of this "pay-out-the-reserves" policy is that it puts the onus directly on other countries to pick their own poison. There is no sense in which the United States could be construed as ramming a dollar standard down their throats. I am firmly convinced that, if the U.S. Government really wanted to negotiate a scheme for limited rate flexibility, it could do so from a position of strength without having to take the drastic step of suspending gold sales and purchases. Under this alternative strategy — which I emphasize is not so much substantively as tactically different — we would, of course, have to take an active leadership in working out the detailed arrangements of such a scheme. But then, despite possible appearances to the contrary at the Fund meetings last week, it is not entirely inappropriate for the largest country in the world to take a strong leadership in such matters.

The main maxim governing U.S. international financial policy in the last decade, it seems to me, has been "he who hesitates is saved". This isn't always such a bad policy. It is the one I am recommending for gold policy, for example. I certainly wish the Defense Department had followed it in 1964 and 1965. On the question of studying in detail and trying to negotiate some further flexibility in exchange rates along the lines of a combined crawling peg and wider band, however, it does seem to me that it is past time to abandon this maxim.

MONETARY CONFERENCE
Melvin Village, New Hampshire
October 8-10, 1969

HAROLD C. BARNETT, Economist
    Federal Reserve Bank of Boston
EUGENE A. BIRNBAUM, Vice President for International Monetary Affairs
    The Chase Manhattan Bank (NA)
W. MICHAEL BLUMENTHAL, President
    Bendix International
DAVID E. BODNER, Assistant Vice President
    Federal Reserve Bank of New York
GEORGE H. BOSSY, Chief, Foreign Research Division
    Federal Reserve Bank of New York
RALPH C. BRYANT, Assistant to the Director, Division of International Finance
    Board of Governors of the Federal Reserve System
JAMES L. BURTLE, Senior Economist
    W. R. Grace Co.
JAMES R. CARTER, Chairman of the Board, Nashua Corporation
    Director, Federal Reserve Bank of Boston
RICHARD E. CAVES, Professor of Economics
    Harvard University
GEORGE H. CHITTENDEN, Senior Vice President
    Morgan Guaranty Trust Company
PHILIP E. COLDWELL, President
    Federal Reserve Bank of Dallas
RICHARD N. COOPER, Frank Altschul Professor of International Economics
    Yale University
ROBERT CORSON, Treasurer
    Foxboro Company
J. HOWARD CRAVEN, Senior Vice President
    Federal Reserve Bank of San Francisco
J. DEWEY DAANE, Member
    Board of Governors of the Federal Reserve System
JAMES S. DUESENBERRY, Professor of Economics, Harvard University
    Director, Federal Reserve Bank of Boston
ROBERT W. EISENMENGER, Senior Vice President and Director of Research
    Federal Reserve Bank of Boston
NORMAN S. FIELEKE, Senior Economist
    Federal Reserve Bank of Boston
J. MARCUS FLEMING, Deputy Director, Research Department
    International Monetary Fund
PETER FOUSEK, Vice President
    Federal Reserve Bank of New York
HENRY H. FOWLER, Partner
    Goldman Sachs and Company
MILTON FRIEDMAN, Paul Snowden Russell Distinguished Service Professor of Economics
    University of Chicago
TILFORD C. GAINES, Vice President and Economist
    Manufacturers Hanover Trust Company
MILTON GILBERT, Economic Adviser
    Bank for International Settlements
GOTTFRIED HABERLER, Galen L. Stone Professor of International Trade
    Harvard University

GEORGE N. HALM, Professor of Economics, Fletcher School of Law and Diplomacy
Tufts University
ALFRED HAYES, President
Federal Reserve Bank of New York
JOHN HEIN, Senior Economist
The National Industrial Conference Board
JOHN B. HENDERSON, Deputy Assistant Secretary for Economic Affairs
U.S. Department of Commerce
J. PHILIP HINSON, Economist
Federal Reserve Bank of Boston
JOHN H. KAREKEN, Professor of Economics, University of Minnesota
Economic Adviser, Federal Reserve Bank of Minneapolis
SAMUEL I. KATZ, Adviser, Division of International Finance
Board of Governors of the Federal Reserve System
CHARLES P. KINDLEBERGER, Professor of Economics
Massachusetts Institute of Technology
FRED H. KLOPSTOCK, Manager, International Research Department
Federal Reserve Bank of New York
LAWRENCE B. KRAUSE, Senior Fellow
The Brookings Institute
MIROSLAV A. KRIZ, Vice President
First National City Bank of New York
JOSEPH G. KVASNICKA, Assistant Vice President and Economist
Federal Reserve Bank of Chicago
WALTHER LEDERER
U.S. Department of the Treasury
JANE S. LITTLE, Financial Analyst
Federal Reserve Bank of Boston
BRUCE K. MACLAURY, Deputy Under Secretary for Monetary Affairs
U.S. Department of the Treasury
SHERMAN J. MAISEL, Member
Board of Governors of the Federal Reserve System
FRANK E. MORRIS, President
Federal Reserve Bank of Boston
BRIAN MURGATROYD
Derby Trust Ltd., London, England
EVELYN M. PARRISH, Economist, Balance of Payments Division, Office of Business
Economics
U.S. Department of Commerce
SIR MAURICE H. PARSONS, Deputy Governor
Bank of England
WILLIAM POOLE, Economist, Division of Research and Statistics
Board of Governors of the Federal Reserve System
JOHN E. REYNOLDS, Associate Director, Division of International Finance
Board of Governors of the Federal Reserve System
W. GORDON ROBERTSON, Co-Chairman of the Board and Chairman of the Executive
Committee, Bangor Punta Corporation
Director, Federal Reserve Bank of Boston
DR. WOLFGANG SCHMITZ, President
Austrian National Bank
FRANCIS H. SCHOTT, Vice President and Associate Economist
The Equitable Life Assurance Society of the United States
ELI SHAPIRO, Professor of Finance, Graduate School of Business Administration
Harvard University

JOHN SIMMEN, Chairman of the Board and Chief Executive Officer, Industrial National
    Bank of Rhode Island
    Director, Federal Reserve Bank of Boston
ROBERT SOLOMON, Adviser to the Board
    Board of Governors of the Federal Reserve System
JOSEPH H. TAGGART, Dean, Graduate School of Business Administration
    New York University
JACK TAYLOR, Senior Economist
    Chas. Pfizer and Co., Inc.
ROBERT TRIFFIN, Frederick William Beinecke Professor of Economics
    Yale University
HERBERT F. WASS, Economist
    Federal Reserve Bank of Boston
JOHN H. WATTS, Banking Executive
    Brown Brothers Harriman and Company
GEORGE H. WILLIS, Deputy to the Assistant Secretary for International Affairs
    U.S. Department of the Treasury
PARKER B. WILLIS, Vice President and Economic Adviser
    Federal Reserve Bank of Boston
RALPH C. WOOD, Adviser, Division of International Finance
    Board of Governors of the Federal Reserve System
PETER ZDRAHAL, Adviser, Secretary to the President
    Austrian National Bank